Supply Chain Financing

Funding the Supply Chain and
the Organization

Supply Chain Financing
Funding the Supply Chain and the Organization

Dale S. Rogers
Arizona State University, USA

Rudolf Leuschner
Rutgers University, USA

Thomas Y. Choi
Arizona State University, USA

NEW JERSEY · LONDON · SINGAPORE · BEIJING · SHANGHAI · HONG KONG · TAIPEI · CHENNAI · TOKYO

Published by

World Scientific Publishing Europe Ltd.

57 Shelton Street, Covent Garden, London WC2H 9HE

Head office: 5 Toh Tuck Link, Singapore 596224

USA office: 27 Warren Street, Suite 401-402, Hackensack, NJ 07601

Library of Congress Cataloging-in-Publication Data

Names: Rogers, Dale, author. | Leuschner, Rudolf, author. | Choi, Thomas Y., author.
Title: Supply chain financing : funding the supply chain and the organization / Dale S. Rogers,
    Arizona State University, USA, Rudolf Leuschner, Rutgers University, USA,
    Thomas Y. Choi, Arizona State University, USA.
Description: New Jersey : World Scientific, 2020. | Includes bibliographical references and index.
Identifiers: LCCN 2019053563 | ISBN 9781786348265 (hardcover) |
    ISBN 9781786348883 (paperback) | ISBN 9781786348272 (ebook) |
    ISBN 9781786348289 (ebook other)
Subjects: LCSH: Business logistics. | Business enterprises--Finance. | Commercial loans.
Classification: LCC HD38.5 .R6354 2020 | DDC 658.7--dc23
LC record available at https://lccn.loc.gov/2019053563

British Library Cataloguing-in-Publication Data
A catalogue record for this book is available from the British Library.

For any available supplementary material, please visit
https://www.worldscientific.com/worldscibooks/10.1142/Q0245#t=suppl

Desk Editors: Balasubramanian/Shi Ying Koe

Typeset by Stallion Press
Email: enquiries@stallionpress.com

Foreword

I have had the privilege of working with the authors of *Supply Chain Financing*: *Funding the Supply Chain and the Organization* for some years now. There has been much research and academic study already done in the overall field of supply chain management. This good work has focused in the past on optimization of the physical supply chain and the benefits a company can achieve as a result. Enhancements and changes seen in the physical supply chain, particularly with improvements in logistics and automation on the procurement (e-invoicing) side, have highlighted the need for overhauling and integrating the financial supply chain side as well to ensure liquidity is amply available to both buyers and their suppliers.

Supply Chain Financing: *Funding the Supply Chain and the Organization* is a culmination of many years of research and analysis by the authors, working with financial services providers to identify emerging trends across the financial supply chain, combining this with insights garnered from the broader trade finance landscape, and assessing the collective impact on how organizations look at supply chain as a concept, a strategy, and a way to manage business. Dale, Rudi, and Tom are well placed to speak on this topic coming from the academic arena in both supply chain and research analysis, and combining their vast knowledge with in-depth work on supply chain and trade finance in the broadest of definitions. This book can easily be used as a "how to" guide on supply chain in the 21st century. It is rich in educational content from the basics of supply chain management to how to structure a global supply chain finance program in today's marketplace, the emergence of fintech providers, and alternative methods of payment, while also offering a view of the future that incorporates new platforms and analytical tools to optimize efficiencies in an organization and increase working capital flows. The student, treasurer, procurement professional, and banker alike can benefit from the information articulated so well in the pages of this book.

Global trade is the cornerstone of commerce and dates back hundreds of years; supply chain, while not commercialized until the mid-1980s, can be referenced going back to the early 1800s. As a banker who has specialized in supply chain finance and trade finance products for 20-plus years, I welcome the continued research and education in this space. As we move forward, it is critical that we maintain a strong foundation in the principals of trade and supply chain while continuing to innovate and grow our global economy. I suspect there will be many exciting updates to this book in the coming years as technology enhancements in areas such as artificial intelligence and blockchain make for continued improvements in both the physical as well as financial supply chain to the betterment of global trade as a whole.

John Monaghan
Global Head — Supply Chain Finance
Citi

John Monaghan is Managing Director in Citi's Treasury and Trade Solutions Group. He has been with Citi for more than 15 years and leads the bank's supply chain finance business globally. Citi is one of the largest providers of supply chain financing services, supporting multinational corporate transactions and providing trade finance products to corporate, financial institutions, and governments around the world.

It is an honor to have been asked to provide a Foreword for this important book. It is my wish that this book will become a favorite and often-used reference for those who influence the everyday practices of supply chain management and corporate finance. Within these pages, decision-makers in corporate disciplines, as well as students of business practices, will find valuable research, guidance, and results.

To those who focus their time and energy in the pursuit of supply chain management excellence, use the contents here as solid business guideposts to aid you in understanding your impact on financial results.

To those who focus their time and energy in the pursuit of corporate financing excellence, use the contents here as solid business guideposts to aid you in understanding how your firm's supplier relationships and contractual terms impact your financial results. Within these pages, you will also find valuable evidence of new and exciting alternative ways of financing your firm through an exceedingly valuable resource — your supply chain partners.

To those who are students of commerce and business in general, use the contents here to advance your understanding about the sometimes delicate, sometimes risky, but always important relationship between suppliers and buyers of goods and services. Applying age-old principles to modern business relationships, and doing so using ever-advancing technologies, is a subject worth your time and energy.

As for my friends Dale Rogers, Rudi Leuschner, and Tom Choi, I can only say. ... I know you needed a lot of help to get this done! Hearty congratulations all around!

Douglas Schoch

Vice President, Treasury Customer Support &
Inhouse Factoring Americas
Siemens Capital Company

Douglas Schoch is responsible for the implementation and growth of the Siemens supply chain finance program in North America. Supply chain finance is an important part of Siemens's initiative to improve working capital and manage supply chain risk. Additionally, Doug heads the Siemens Credit Warehouse team responsible for providing transparency to customer exposure and credit risk management services for Siemens companies throughout the Americas.

Is there a company out there that would not benefit from an improved cash position? Many companies must make choices based on their ability or even a key supplier's ability to fund certain initiatives. They may miss a timely opportunity or, even worse, disrupt an operation due to lack of sufficient funding. Because so many of these companies find themselves in highly competitive industries, they can't afford to miss too many opportunities or certainly, to disrupt operations. In fact, they are driven to pursue every possible angle to improve efficiency across every aspect of their business. If they don't, the competition surely will, and we all know how that story ends.

In an effort to keep pace, companies spend much of their days mining traditional areas of continuous improvement, over and over again. Can we take a few precious seconds out of a production process? Can we eliminate a step in our distribution network? Is there a lower cost shipping method? Is there a benefit to outsourcing a particular function?

These are all noble pursuits that should never cease. Even small incremental improvements can add up to the advantage that a firm needs to stay competitive in the marketplace. Yet, as we chase these incremental improvements, we tend to overlook some non-traditional opportunities that can provide a significant benefit to our companies and our supply base. Supply chain financing is one of those often-overlooked opportunities.

Most companies rely on a strong, stable supply base to support their goals for developing cutting-edge, new technology and products. They need suppliers to invest in production facilities and equipment to facilitate growth. At the same time, it is absolutely imperative that their supply bases maintain a financially stable position so that they can continuously supply the materials, parts, or services companies need to keep operations going. So, why wouldn't companies pursue all possible options to help their suppliers help them to fund their own goals?

The first time I really began to understand supply chain financing was during a lecture by Dr. Dale Rogers at a CAPS Research event. I had heard a little about supply chain financing in other forums, but I had conjured up images of some kind of payment term trickery that would leave our suppliers in a difficult leverage position. As I talked with others in my profession, I found a similar lack of knowledge and understanding. Worse yet, like me, others had filled in the blanks with misinformation and were not seriously investigating this approach within their companies.

Fortunately, as I listened to Dr. Rogers speak, my viewpoint opened up. Like so many other experiences with the professionals involved in CAPS Research, I began to see the possibilities. Supply chain financing would not put our suppliers in a difficult leverage position. In fact, it has the potential to help fund our suppliers' operations, as well as our own!

On that day, Dr. Rogers leveraged his unique ability to take very complex topics and boil them down to their essence. In this book, Dr. Rogers, Dr. Choi, and Dr. Leuschner team up to do the same but in an even more comprehensive way. They dig deep into the topic of supply chain financing and lay it out an easily understandable format. They simplify the topic without compromising the depth or the breadth of the tool and its potential uses. But, they don't stop there. Rogers, Choi, and Leuschner cover a range of related topics to ensure that the reader walks away with a thorough understanding of the emerging trends in the crossroads between procurement and finance.

In my 32 years of procurement and supply chain experience in the auto industry for Honda, I've read a lot of books and heard a lot of theories on how we can improve our business. Publications from long-time practitioners tend to "tell it like it is" but sometimes lack supporting data or sound research. Scholars and researchers on the other hand may fill the reader to the brim with theory, while coming up short on practical application. This book does both!

Dale Rogers, Tom Choi, and Rudi Leuschner have carried out solid research based on real-world data collected from numerous companies and then put it into an actionable form. When you've read this book, you will be fully equipped to gather the right people and ask the right questions to assess the value of supply chain financing in any company in any industry. Powerful stuff!

Whether you are a professor, or a student interested in developing your knowledge base, or a supply chain or finance professional that is looking for a new opportunity to add value to your company, this book will serve you well. Join the ranks of the few who truly understand these cutting-edge tools and are equipped to help companies get stronger and compete in new, non-traditional ways.

Tom Lake
Executive Vice President
Honda Canada, Inc.

Tom Lake is Senior Vice President at Honda North America. He is responsible for supply management.

Preface

In June of 2016, the three of us published in the online *Harvard Business Review* an article entitled "The Rise of FinTech in Supply Chains."[1] That article introduced a new breed of companies called *Fintechs* and their involvement in supply chain financing (SCF). Subsequent online comments ranged from the criticism of SCF potentially being unethical to the inevitability of the rise of fintech companies and SCF practices. Such diverse comments pressed us to engage in this book project. The bulk of the foundational knowledge behind this book has come from a CAPS Research report published in 2016.[2]

Traditionally, supply chain management has been summarized into three major activities: the terms *source*, *make*, and *deliver* are often used synonymously with the topic. Recently, there has appeared a new purpose for supply chain management — *to fund*. With advances in technological development, the supply chain has become the cheapest source of cash in many organizations. Supply chain financing enables managers to improve the company's balance sheet and income statement. Using its financial strength, a buying firm can fund the supply chain. In addition, various financial instruments can be used to mitigate risks in the supply chain.

---

[1] Rogers, Dale; Rudolf Leuschner & Thomas Choi. "The Rise of FinTech in Supply Chains," *Harvard Business Review*, June 22, 2016, https://hbr.org/2016/06/the-rise-of-fintech-in-supply-chains.

[2] Rogers, Dale; Rudolf Leuschner & Thomas Choi (2016). *Supply Chain Financing: Funding the Supply Chain and the Organization*, Tempe, AZ: CAPS Research.

Overall, SCF complements standard corporate finance activities by reducing the firm's reliance on other sources of funding, thereby reducing costs and ensuring that retained earnings and profitability are maximized.

According to what we have learned in the past five years, supply chain financing is an important frontier in managing the supply chain. Not only have banks and buyers provided significant liquidity to large companies' suppliers, but they also have enabled significant transactional efficiency in terms of payments and documentation. There has been considerable innovation in the SCF realm, which allows firms using those solutions to provide liquidity to the supply chain. This innovation has manifested in the rapidly expanding financial technology industry, known as "fintech" firms. They have developed streamlined processes to manage financial flows and develop alternative sources of funding. The term *supply chain financing* has appeared in relation to products that are offered by financial institutions and third-party providers.

This book highlights areas of collaboration, especially involving the corporate finance function and treasury, in addition to suppliers and customers. We recognize an opportunity for supply chain management professionals to expand their role into critical financial issues, as they can significantly alter how relationships with suppliers are managed and improve both the financial position of their firm and their suppliers' firms. Some of the tools presented in this book can bring significant value to the organization because they provide access to liquidity, which is often difficult to access otherwise.

About the Authors

Dale S. Rogers is the ON Semiconductor Professor of Business at the Supply Chain Management Department at Arizona State University. He is also the Director of the Frontier Economies Logistics Lab and the Co-Director of the Internet Edge Supply Chain Lab ASU. Dale is the Leader in Supply Chain Finance, Sustainability, and Reverse Logistics Practices for ILOS — Instituto de Logística e-Supply Chain in Rio de Janeiro, Brazil. In 2012, he became the first academic to receive the International Warehouse and Logistics Association Distinguished Service Award in its 130-year history. He is a Board Advisor to Flexe, Enterra Solutions, and Droneventory; is a Founding Board Member of the Global Supply Chain Resiliency Council, Reverse Logistics, and Sustainability Council; and serves on the Board of Directors for the Organización Mundial de Ciudades y Plataformas Logísticas.

Dale is a Leading Researcher in the fields of Reverse Logistics, Sustainable Supply Chain Management, Supply Chain Finance, and Secondary Markets, and has published in leading journals of the supply chain and logistics fields. He has been a principal investigator on research grants from numerous organizations. He is a Senior Editor at *Rutgers Business Journal*, area Editor at *Annals of Management Science*, and

Associate Editor of the *Journal of Business Logistics* and the *Journal of Supply Chain Management.*

He has made more than 300 presentations to professional organizations and has been a faculty member in numerous executive education programs at universities in the United States, China, Europe, and South America as well as at major corporations and professional organizations. Dr. Rogers has been a consultant to several companies, a principal investigator on research grants from numerous organizations.

 **Rudolf Leuschner** is a tenured Associate Professor at the Department of Supply Chain Management and the Program Director for the online Master of Science in the Supply Chain Management program at Rutgers Business School. He is at the forefront of online education as the Faculty Coordinator for Distance and Online Learning and the creator of the Supply Chain Management MOOC specialization.

His research focuses on the end-to-end supply chain and the integration of its three primary flows: products, information, and finances. Specifically, in the new field of Supply Chain Finance, he has been active in developing relevant insights for academic and practitioner audiences. He co-developed the Rutgers Business School Payment Practices Index which ranks retailers' performance. He received his Ph.D. with a major in Logistics and a minor in Marketing from The Ohio State University. His work has appeared among others in the *Journal of Supply Chain Management, Journal of Business Logistics, Decision Sciences*, the *Journal of Business Ethics, Harvard Business Review*, and *Rutgers Business Review*. He has been a frequent speaker at academic as well as practitioner conferences. His teaching interests at the undergraduate, graduate, and executive education levels are on the topics of Supply Chain Strategy, Supply Chain Finance, and Demand Management.

 **Thomas Y. Choi** is Professor of Supply Chain Management at W.P. Carey School of Business, Arizona State University. He leads the study of the upstream side of supply chains, where a buying company interfaces with many suppliers organized in various forms of networks. He has published in the *Academy of Management Executive, Decision Sciences, Harvard Business Review, Journal of Operations Management, Production and Operations Management*, and others.

He co-directs the Complex Adaptive Supply Networks Research Accelerator, a research group made up of scholars from around the world interested in supply networks and complexity. He has worked with numerous corporations including LG Electronics, Samsung, Toyota, Volvo, and the U.S. Department of Energy. He has served as Harold E. Fearon Chair of Purchasing Management and Executive Director of CAPS Research, a joint venture between Arizona State University and the Institute for Supply Management from 2014 to 2019. He served as co-EIC for the *Journal of Operations Management* from 2011 to 2014. In 2012, he was recognized as the Distinguished Operations Management Scholar by the OM Division at the Academy of Management. Since 2018, he has been listed as a Highly Cited Researcher by Clarivate Analytics for having "multiple highly cited papers that rank in the top 1 percent by citations for field and year in Web of Science."

Acknowledgments

The authors and CAPS Research would like to acknowledge and thank the many companies and professionals within those firms that participated in this research. Although some of these firms asked to remain anonymous due to the sensitive nature of their supply chain financing strategies, they generously and openly took part in the interview process. Their experiences and insights greatly added to the depth and breadth of the research.

Contents

List of Figures

Appendix A

Appendix C

List of Tables

Chapter 8

Chapter 9

Appendix C

Chapter 1

Introduction

What is Supply Chain Financing?

A third-party logistics (3PL) company was facing extended payables from its customer. This 3PL was working for a large electronics manufacturer customer, which moved its payment terms to "end of week + 80 days." The 3PL, as a supplier of logistics services, was hiring trucking firms to haul freight for this customer, and the trucking companies demanded 30-day terms. This 3PL supplier also had a large debt hangover due to a substantial acquisition it had made a few years prior. The 3PL faced a financial dilemma: it did not want to act as a bank and needed to closely manage its working capital. To overcome the dilemma, it signed up with a major financial institution to do a supply chain financing (SCF) program through the customer's SCF program. After an invoice was approved by the customer and the 80-days + some-fraction-of-the-current-week clock started, it was able to get paid quickly — within 10–15 days. It was even able to use this quicker payment to pay down the debt left over from its acquisition. As this example illustrates, SCF is an initiative to reduce costs, improve working capital, and manage risk more tightly. The theme of this book explores this concept and details how firms can leverage their supply chains to help improve their financial position.

As large manufacturers have tightened their supply chains and extended payment terms, their suppliers have had difficulty financing their operations. This difficulty in obtaining funding has severe implications on cash flow, working capital, and profitability, and it can sometimes lead to bankruptcies and supply disruptions. With capital often difficult to obtain, firms must develop more creative ways to help finance their diverse and increasingly underfunded supply bases. While factoring and reverse factoring of inventories and receivables have often been called SCF, the topic as we define it goes far beyond those practices. Broadly speaking, SCF is how firms are funded through their supply chains and how they fund their supply chains. To the best of our knowledge, there is little published research on the topic of SCF in the supply chain literature, and the topic is in the early stages of development. SCF will have an increasingly valuable and important impact on all entities in the supply chain in the future.

To meet the needs of global supply chains that have become increasingly complex, new financial infrastructures are developing to support these evolving networks of firms. Financial service firms, including large banks and specialized financial institutions, have developed services to support suppliers that require liquidity and working capital. An executive at a major financial institution estimated that his firm performs $2.2 trillion per day in trade finance transactions, which typically includes loans to suppliers to buy raw materials, components, and finished goods. Given that the 2017 US gross domestic product (GDP) was approximately $19 trillion, this is a substantial amount of activity designed primarily for supporting procurement operations around the world.

SCF is larger than simply finance plus supply chain management. That is, there is a symbiotic effect in the combination of supply chain management and finance that makes the whole greater than the sum of the parts. SCF involves utilizing the supply chain to develop savings, generate profits, and efficiently manage assets to fund the firm. It includes working on improving both the income statements and the balance sheets for a firm and its suppliers. The supply chain can be a source of funds for the firm; a firm can use its supply base to generate funds and act as a source of funding for the organization. Additionally, helping one's suppliers fund themselves is an integral part of SCF. Later in this book, we describe an example of how one company uses its balance sheet and business acumen in this manner.

Our perspective on SCF can be captured in a simple sentence as follows:

SCF is using the supply chain to fund the organization, and using the organization to fund the supply chain.

Ultimately, SCF involves utilizing the supply chain to develop savings, generate profits, and efficiently manage assets to fund the firm, whether buying or selling. It includes working to improve both the income statement and the balance sheet for a buying firm and its suppliers. SCF can bring structure and discipline to the financial portion of the supply chain, which can in turn improve the physical supply chain. It can reduce variability of payments in the supply chain and therefore can reduce the need for additional cash to alleviate uncertainty.

SCF enables a firm's managers to improve the balance sheet to fund the supply chain and to use financial instruments to mitigate risks in the supply chain. In addition, SCF complements standard corporate finance activities by reducing a firm's reliance on other sources of funding, thereby reducing costs to ensure that profitability and retained earnings are maximized.

The supply chain has three major flows: product/service, information, and finances. As supply chains increase in complexity those three flows can become disjointed. The three flows often move through different intermediaries. Products might be routed through 3PL firms or transportation and warehousing providers. Services might be routed through third-party service firms (e.g., talent search, online data processing, ad agencies, etc.). Information is transmitted through the cloud and information service providers. Payments flow through multiple banks and other financial intermediaries.

In general, SCF has the strong potential to be a win for both the buyer and the seller, with numerous additional benefits such as providing significant liquidity, enforcing discipline in the approval of invoices, and taking the variability out of the timing of payments. While there have been some misconceptions about the viability of such programs, we have seen no evidence that there are significant barriers to the implementation of such programs, such as the accounting treatment.

Firms have constrained access to external capital because buying firms have tightened their supply chains. Suppliers have had difficulty in financing their operations to supply these larger firms. The struggle to obtain funding can increase the cost of business and sometimes lead to shortages and even bankruptcies. Large corporations and small suppliers alike have had to develop methods to finance their diverse and sometimes underfunded supply chains. Key financial tools have ranged from commercial credit cards to fintech-enabled dynamic discounting and reverse factoring. These topics are covered in this book.

Global Impact of Supply Chain Financing

Global trade outside the United States has been expanding, and SCF practices are evolving with that expansion. There has been a dramatic shift of trade flows into emerging markets that desperately need capital to supply the developing world. Small- and medium-sized businesses in these emerging markets are often underfunded. As their supply chains expand so does the need for readily accessible, low-cost financing. Non-investment-grade companies and small-to-medium enterprises (SMEs) find it difficult to finance their working capital requirements as buying firms have tightened their supply chains; this can be particularly true for smaller suppliers in emerging economies such as India. The result is that there is a significant credit arbitrage between large firms in established markets and their suppliers in emerging economies. Large corporations have been forced to develop methods to finance their diverse and sometimes underfunded supply chains. Working capital management needs to be part of buying firms' strategies when developing suppliers. Working capital solutions can assist buyers to monetize these arbitrage opportunities while assisting their suppliers. In general, buyers and suppliers typically have conflicting objectives, and strong buyers tend to take advantage of weaker suppliers. The use of SCF tools has the potential to contribute around $400 billion to Western European economies while reducing overall costs and decreasing supply chain disruption.[1] These tools could also

---

[1] Kristina, D., Diederik, V. Fabian, N., Mark, L., Elco, R., Laurent, P., Erica, M. and Laurent, F. (2014). "Innovative Business Models: Supply Chain Finance." *Business Innovation Observatory*, Contract No. 190/PP/ENT/CIP/12/C/N03C01.

give access to capital for small- and medium-sized enterprises and allow access to new export markets by making them more liquid. In the long run, however, only the solutions that are mutually beneficial for buyers and suppliers will work.

As mentioned earlier, there are three major flows in the supply chain: product/service, information, and finances. Most existing supply chain literature focuses on the first two, and only little attention has been paid to the financial side of supply chain management. However, it is the financial flows that often exert the greatest influence on the development of the structure of supply chains. In many cases, financial flows determine the structure and complexity of the supply chain. Typically, supply chains are not designed merely to facilitate product or information flows. Instead, they are designed to optimize the financial objectives of a firm. Generally, financial structures and issues drive the structure of the supply chain and operational methods.

When a firm is considering adopting a SCF program, it is, by definition, inter-organizational. Several groups get involved in developing SCF programs including treasury, the CFO organization, and the CPO organization. When it comes to implementation, systems and information technology (IT) need to participate. Once the program is mandated, the buying firm's procurement organization is most likely to drive the implementation. Usually the goal of the procurement organization is to improve the firms' working capital measures and extend payment terms to suppliers. When developing an SCF program, it is imperative that it is done in a collaborative manner, so that all the messaging is accurate and acceptable to the supply chain. While suppliers may actually benefit from a standardized set of extended payment terms, it is unlikely that they will initially accept it without concerns.

Chapter 2

Financial Components of the Supply Chain

Introduction

In this chapter, we describe the background of critical elements and considerations that affect the development and implementation of supply chain financing (SCF) strategies and practices. We discuss how the purpose of the supply chain has evolved over time, and how trade finance in general enables activity in the supply chain.

The Transformed Purpose of the Supply Chain

The supply chain is more than just about "source, make, deliver." A critical departure from this prevalent perspective begins with observing that the cheapest source of cash actually resides within the supply chain. We propose to add "fund" to "source, make, deliver."

As supply chains increase in complexity, the flows of product/service, information, and finances become disjointed. These flows move through separate channels and different intermediaries. Products might be routed through third-party logistics firms. Information travels through the cloud. Payments flow through multiple banks and other intermediaries. The banks assist with payment flow integration across a firm's supply chain. For example, banks will facilitate payments to suppliers and service providers in foreign countries, so a buying firm does not have to contend with local regulations. The bank system simplifies the audit, approval, and payment of freight-related expenses by automating the entire supply chain process. Transactions take place online, from the pre-payment audits, to review and negotiation with shippers, to expense allocation, and more — and the payment takes place in cyberspace. All these transactions can be separate from the physical movement of goods. This means that a Chinese trucking company can deliver a shipment to an American subsidiary plant in China, and the entire transaction could take place in a computer in New Jersey in the United States.

It would be a serious blow to major multinational corporations (MNCs) if global banks decide to stop offering SCF services. According to a recent article in *The Wall Street Journal*, "Huawei, active in about 170 countries, relies on international banks to manage cash, finance trade and fund its operations and investments. For more than a decade, HSBC, Standard Chartered, and Citigroup plugged Huawei into the global financial system as it entered new markets, providing it with everything from foreign currencies to bond funding from Western investors."[1] The business services these banks would provide include "providing regional and global cash pools that free up excess cash in local Huawei units and let it pay suppliers in multiple currencies." How a major MNC like Huawei will navigate through this increasing financial complexity remains to be seen. However, it is clear supply chains are global with increasing financial footprints.

Ensuring adequate liquidity is of paramount concern for all executives involved in supply chain management. SCF can bring structure and discipline to the financial portion of the supply chain. We believe this financial structure and discipline can actually improve the physical supply chain and make it function better. It can reduce variability, create capacity, and make it easier to manage. Better financial management of both payables and receivables can allow buyers and suppliers to invest in initiatives that they would not have been able to otherwise. SCF allows increased capacity for both because it frees up working capital. Unlocking working capital allows a firm to better handle ongoing expenses. If a firm can extend the

---

[1] Patrick, M. and Julie, S. (2018). "Some Global Banks Break Ties With Huawei." *The Wall Street Journal*, December 20, 2018. Retrieved from www.wsj.com/articles/some-global-banks-break-ties-with-huawei-11545321306?mod=hp_lead_pos4.

amount of cash it has, it can use that money to help buy a new plant or equipment, lower the need for long-term financing, and make other investments. In this regard, SCF can inject liquidity into the system so that trapped cash can be unlocked and converted from working capital into cash. According to CAPS Research, a consumer packaged goods firm has been able to increase capacity by embarking on an SCF program in recent years.[2] Its intent was to unlock working capital, turn it into cash, and use that cash to fund investments in new markets and opportunities. In some cases, unlocking working capital has resulted in increased cash of $100–200 million on an annual basis. The same CAPS Research report illustrates how suppliers are able to get cash early or at the time of their own choosing with minimal penalty because the early payment is facilitated by the larger and (presumably) financially more stable buying company's credit rating.

The Enabling Role of Trade Finance

Trade finance consists of "using trade credit (accounts receivable) as collateral and/or the purchase of insurance against the possibility of trade credit defaults."[3] In traditional trade finance contracts, exporters obtain working capital loans, credit lines, discounted prepayments, or credit default insurance based on foreign purchase orders or credit guarantees provided by the importer's bank.

Globally, trade finance is large, and it is estimated that about 90 percent of firm-to-firm transactions involve some form of trade finance. These are typically short-term flows of money in and out of a business. Furthermore, the overall global market for trade finance, including credit and insurance, is estimated to be more than $12 trillion per year.[4] A senior

---

[2]Rogers, D., Leuschner, R. and Choi, T. (2016). *Supply Chain Financing: Funding the Supply Chain and the Organization*, CAPS Research, Tempe, AZ.

[3]Ahn, J., Amiti, M. and Weinstein, D. E. (2011). "Trade Finance and the Great Trade Collapse." *American Economic Review: Papers & Proceedings*, 101(3), 298–302. Retrieved from www.aeaweb.org/articles.php?doi=10.1257/aer.101.3.298.

[4]Auboin, M. (2009). Boosting the Availability of Trade Finance in the Current Crisis: Background Analysis for a Substantial G20 Package. CEPR Policy Insight No. 35, Centre for Economic Policy Research, London.

executive at a large financial institution estimated that $2.2 trillion of trade finance went through his firm each day. Without trade finance, supply chains and the world economy at large would quickly grind to a halt.

Overview of Financial Statements

A recent article published in *The New York Times*, entitled "Why Apple Is the Future of Capitalism," describes how Apple plays its financial game differently from other companies.[5] The article contends that Apple plays the cash flow game rather than the profit maximization game. To fully appreciate such a strategy by Apple, one should understand a few basic concepts of financial statements. In this section, several basic financial statements are described. This is an elementary review of such statements; it may be that the reader is already quite familiar with these financial terms as they are utilized in most business operations around the world.

Balance Sheet: Assets, Liabilities, and Cash

A balance sheet is a report of the financial position and health of a firm on a specific date, which is typically the end of an accounting period such as a quarter or fiscal year. It depicts the assets, liabilities, and shareholders' equity of the firm. Assets are resources that are owned by the firm and are intended to provide benefits in the future. From a supply chain management point of view, the key asset on the balance sheet is inventory. Much of the work that a supply chain manager needs to complete relates to the inventory asset. As supply chain managers know, there are different types of inventories that need to be managed. The five basic types of inventories include the following:

1. raw materials (Raw),
2. work-in-progress (WIP),
3. finished goods (FGI),
4. packaging materials,
5. maintenance, repair, and operating (MRO) supplies.

---

[5]Desai, M. (2018). "Why Apple is the Future of Capitalism." *The New York Times*, August 8, 2018. Retrieved from www.nytimes.com/2018/08/06/opinion/apple-trillion-market-cap.html.

Other inventory classifications that cut across the categories listed above can include goods in transit, buffer stock, anticipatory stock, decoupling stock, and cycle stock.

The responsibility for managing inventory is often spread across the supply chain management organization and finance. While finance managers do not typically become involved in inventory management decisions except for things such as write-downs or a few other duties, supply chain managers typically manage the bulk of inventory management operations. While inventory is a key component on the balance sheet, it is also a part of working capital management. The responsibility for working capital management typically resides in finance. Therefore, because inventory management is a key component of working capital management, both the finance and supply chain organizations may have oversight. For example, the inventory turnover ratio has been utilized to measure the velocity of inventory movement. Inventory turnover became popular following the advent of just-in-time (now referred to as "lean" supply chain management). Inventory turnover can be calculated using different methods depending on the data that are available. The most common method is cost of goods sold (COGS) divided by average inventories. If average inventory value is unavailable because a balance sheet is used to determine the inventory value number, then ending inventory level at COGS value should be utilized. In some cases, where the firm is not publicly held and financial data are difficult to determine, sales in revenue dollars are used instead of COGS. This drastically overestimates the inventory turnover ratio. Inventory turns are considered an "activity utilization ratio" and are a metric to indicate how efficiently a business is using its assets.

Other activity utilization ratios within working capital include receivables turnover, average collection period, and payables turnover. Often, managers use other measures related to these activity utilization ratios. These other measures can include the following:

- days of inventory outstanding (DIO),
- days of sales outstanding (DSO),
- days of payables outstanding (DPO).

These ratios inform the manager of the size of working capital components in terms of the number of days that it typically takes to completely turn over inventory, receive payments that are outstanding, and pay supplier firms. These ratios are the three components of the cash conversion cycle (CCC) which is described in Chapter 3.

Income Statement

The income statement presents the financial results of a business for an accounting period. The accounting period may be a month, a quarter, or a fiscal year. It begins with sales and works down to net income and earnings per share. It is different from the balance sheet in that it describes amounts of revenue generated and expenses incurred by the firm, as well as any profits or losses. It is also referred to as the "P&L" or profit and loss statement. Financial performance is measured through a summary of how the business incurs revenues and expenses through both operating and non-operating activities. It depicts the net profit or loss incurred over a specific accounting period.

The majority of expenses related to managing the supply chain will be documented in the income statement. These costs would include all of the portions of COGS (or cost of revenue) that are part of the transformation and distribution of products and services.

Income statements may not be consistent among firms, or even sometimes between divisions of a single firm. There is not a standard form in the GAAP accounting standards for how the income statement must be formatted. However, income statements generally contain at least the following elements:

- revenue,
- expenses (including those from operations, purchasing, distribution, and tax),
- post-tax profit or loss for discontinued operations and for the disposal of these operations,
- profit/loss,
- total income.

There are generally two parts of an income statement: operating and non-operating revenue and expenses. The operating portion of the income statement describes revenues and expenses that result from normal business operations. The non-operating section includes revenues and expenses from activities that are not a standard part of a firm's operations.

Firms utilize the income statement for the calculation of many financial ratios such as return on equity, return on assets, gross profit, operating profit, earnings before interest and taxes (EBIT), and earnings before interest, taxes, depreciation, and amortization (EBITDA).

Cash Flow Statement

The statement of cash flow shows the changes in a firm's cash position during a specific period. The change is calculated as follows:

$$\text{Change in cash} = \text{cash flows from operating activities}$$
$$\pm \text{ cash flows from investing activities}$$
$$\pm \text{ cash flows from financing activities.}$$

Most cash flows from operating activities come out of improvements in managing the supply chain. Cash flows from operating (CFO) activities are calculated as follows:

$$\text{CFO} = (\text{cash from customers} + \text{interest} + \text{dividends}) - (\text{cash to suppliers and employees} + \text{interest paid} + \text{income taxes paid}).$$

If an analyst or a supply chain manager does not have access to the above elements from the supplier's accounting systems, these figures can be estimated from the income statement or the balance sheet using the following formula:

$$\text{CFO} = \text{net income} + \text{depreciation} + \text{amortization} + \text{other non-cash charges}$$
$$\pm \text{ increase/decrease in working capital.}$$

These cash flows can be very important in valuing a firm. The typical method for valuing a firm is through the use of a calculation of EBITDA which is the sum of:

$$\text{EBITDA} = \text{net income} + \text{interest} + \text{depreciation} + \text{amortization.}$$

Typically, the basis for selling or acquiring a firm is EBITDA. A firm that wants to acquire another company will often use a valuation formula that utilizes a multiple of EBITDA as the purchase price. For example, if a firm was going to purchase a third-party logistics firm, the purchase price for acquiring it might be 10 times EBITDA in a good market. In a recession the purchase price of acquiring the firm might be as low as five or six times EBITDA.

Cash

Our observation is that firms are seeking to increase their cash holdings as much as possible. Lie and Liu (2018) found that US non-financial companies held "$1.68 trillion in cash at the end of 2015, double the $815 billion amount they held in 2007. Furthermore, Harford *et al.* (2014) show that average cash holdings for US firms increased steadily from about 12 percent in the 1980s to 14 percent in the 1990s and 18 percent in the 2000s."[6] This is a substantial amount of cash holdings. The overall pattern has been that cash holdings have significantly increased over the last 30 years. The average cash ratio (*cash and cash equivalents/current liabilities*) increased by an average of 0.5 percent per year between 1980 and 2006, and that increase has further accelerated since the Great Recession of 2009.[7,8]

Firms need to accumulate cash for several different reasons. One reason is that firms need cash for expenditures in research and development. Another reason has been the difficulty in repatriation of funds from a low-tax market to a higher tax market. For example, up until 2018 the corporate tax rate in the United States was approximately 35 percent.

---

[6]Lie, E. and Liu, Y. (2018). "Corporate Cash Holdings and Acquisitions: Corporate Cash Holdings and Acquisitions." *Financial Management*, 47(1), 159–173. Retrieved from https://doi.org/10.1111/fima.12185.

[7]Bates, T. W., Chang, C. H. and Chi, J. D. (2012). Why Has the Value of Cash Increased Over Time? *SSRN Working Paper Series*.

[8]Bates, T. W., Kahle, K. M. and Schulz, R. M. (2009). "Why Do US Firms Hold So Much More Cash Than They Used to?" *The Journal of Finance*, 64(5), 1985–2021.

That high rate made it difficult to bring revenue back to the United States from abroad.

This has significant influence on the use of SCF techniques that have gained in popularity over the past several years. For example, there are four important points regarding the observation that cash holdings have increased: inventories have fallen; cash flow risk for firms has increased; capital expenditures have declined as firms outsource more; and finally, fueled by increased cash holdings, R&D expenditures have increased.[9]

Working Capital

Working capital is a metric that represents a firm's short-term financial viability and the efficiency with which the firm manages its short-term assets and liabilities. Short term is generally defined as 12 months or less. Working capital is typically calculated as:

Working capital = current assets − current liabilities.

Another related measure is the working capital ratio:

Working capital ratio = current assets/current liabilities.

The working capital ratio indicates whether a firm has enough short-term capital to cover its short-term debt. On the one hand, measures below 1.00 indicate insufficient working capital. On the other hand, ratios larger than 2.00 are seen as inefficient because they signify a reluctance to invest in the business. The sources of those metrics are explained in Table 1. The working capital ratio can be tracked over time to reveal potential issues regarding the financial health of the firm. Firms can improve working capital by accelerating receivables from customers, delaying payables to suppliers, or liquidating inventory. In general, working capital provides investors with an indication of the firm's operational efficiency.

---

[9] *Ibid.*

Table 1:   Balance Sheet Items Used to Calculate Working Capital

Current Assets (Assets that can be converted into cash within the current fiscal year)	
Cash and Cash Equivalents	The value of a firm's cash holdings or holdings that can be converted into cash quickly. Examples include cash in bank accounts and other marketable securities such as certificates of deposit, commercial paper, banker's acceptances, treasury bills, and other money market instruments.
Accounts Receivable	Payments owed by customers for goods and/or services.
Inventory	Raw materials, work-in-progress, and finished goods that are ready or will be ready for sale.
Prepaid Expenses	Payments that have already been made for goods and services to be received in the near future. Examples include yearly advance payments for insurance policies that have not yet been used.
Current Liabilities (Debts or obligations to be repaid within the current fiscal year)	
Short-term Debt	Debt that is due within the current fiscal year, such as bank loans taken out by a company.
Accounts Payable	Payments owed to suppliers for goods and/or services.
Accrued Liabilities	An expense that has been incurred but has not yet paid. Typical examples are payments due at a specified date to cover payroll taxes.

Ratios and Heuristics

Next, we will briefly review several important financial ratios and heuristics relevant to supply chain management.

Profitability Ratios

Profitability ratios can be classified into two general categories: margin ratios and return ratios. Among margin ratios, there are typically gross profit margin, operating profit margin, and cash flow margin. They highlight a firm's ability to convert revenues into profits. Return ratios show a firm's ability to convert profit into returns for shareholders. The following are descriptions of a few commonly used ratios.

- **Gross profit margin.** Gross profit margin is calculated as gross profit divided by revenue. It shows how effective a company is in selling the goods and services it produces into profit. A higher gross profit margin ratio is thought to be a sign of higher efficiency of core operations, (i.e., ability to cover operating expenses, fixed costs, dividends, and depreciation) while providing earnings to the company. A low profit margin can be a reflection of high COGS (e.g., inefficient purchasing, low selling prices, low sales, strong market competition, or ineffective sales promotion policies).
- **Operating profit margin.** Another profitability ratio, operating profit, is calculated as a ratio of earnings divided by sales before income tax is applied. Firms with higher operating profit margins may have efficient strategies for paying off fixed costs and interest on debt (which differentiates operating profit from net profit). They are considered to be more robust to market volatility, and have the ability to compete on price more easily than their counterparts with lower operating profit margin. This metric is typically used to evaluate the efficiency of a firm's management.
- **Cash flow margin.** Cash flow measures the ability of the firm to convert sales into cash. The higher the ratio, the more cash is available to pay suppliers, dividends, utilities, and service debt, as well as to invest in capital assets. Low or negative cash flow margin, on the contrary, indicates that although the business is generating revenues, it may still be unprofitable. To make up the difference, the firm may need to issue debt or equity to continue operations. Interestingly, in a time of recession, it has been found that firms reduce the number of suppliers they utilize. As firms emerge from the recession they begin to increase their numbers of suppliers.[10]

---

[10]Huff, J. and Rogers, D. S. (2015). "Funding the Organization Through Supply Chain Finance: A Longitudinal Investigation." *Supply Chain Forum: An International Journal*, 16(3), 4–17.

Return Ratios

- **Return on assets (ROA).** ROA measures the percentage of net earnings compared to the company's total assets. In other words, the ratio shows how much after-tax profit a firm generates for every dollar of assets it holds, which is similar to the asset intensity of a business. For example, in the 3PL industry, there are asset-based and non-asset-based companies. CH Robinson is a trucking company that does not own any trucks. Instead it utilizes trucks that are the assets of other firms and makes those available to shippers that need those to move products. Some consider non-asset-based models superior because the firm has more flexibility and higher ROA.
- **Return on equity (ROE).** ROE is calculated as the percentage of net income relative to stockholders' equity. In other words, it is the rate of return on the equity that investors have provided. ROE is carefully monitored by analysts and investors. A high ratio is often viewed as a reason to buy a stock. When firms have a higher return on equity they are more capable of generating cash through their own operations, which makes them less dependent on debt financing.
- **Return on invested capital (ROIC).** ROIC measures return generated by all providers of capital, including bondholders and shareholders. It is more inclusive than ROE as it includes returns on capital by bondholders. In its calculation, EBIT is used because it represents earnings generated before deducting interest expenses, and therefore represents earnings available to all investors, rather than just to shareholders. The simplified ROIC formula is as follows:

$$\text{ROIC} = \text{EBIT} \times (1 - \text{tax rate})/(\text{value of debt} + \text{value of equity}).$$

Chapter 3

Financial Tools

Impact of SCM on Profitability of the Firm

The bulk of a firm's assets are found within the supply chain. In this regard, the supply chain has always had a major impact on profitability. Manufacturing and distribution assets make up a large percentage of Fortune 500 company assets that produce products. Inventory is often the most important portion of a firm's assets that the supply chain organization manages.

Asset Valuation

Asset valuation is a process of assessing the values of assets in a firm. This can include real property such as plants, property, and equipment, or any other item of worth that has been capitalized. Capitalization means that the item is placed on the balance sheet as a corporate asset. Asset valuation includes a process of assessing assets that produce cash flows. Asset valuation is typically performed before the purchase or a sale of an asset or before insurance is purchased for that asset. For example, if a firm acquires a plant, a beneficial asset valuation will be conducted not only so the purchase price can be established but also so that the proper amount of insurance can be acquired.

Much of finance is centered around asset valuation. These assets can include stocks, bonds, buildings, equipment, and intangible assets such as goodwill, brands, and occasionally even labor. Often, the firm's assets are clustered in and around the supply chain. As a result, supply chain management has a large impact on the value of assets.

When analysts are valuing a firm, they typically look at both the asset's book value and its market value. The book value is normally lower than market value because assets are placed on the balance sheet at their historical cost. An asset value is typically developed by comparing that specific asset to similar ones and then estimating likely cash flows that will be derived from that asset. The cost of acquiring a similar asset, replacement costs, and depreciation methods can also be used to value assets. One of the most common ways of valuing assets is based on estimated future cash flows.

"Should-Cost" Modeling

Should-cost modeling is a tool that many supply management professionals utilize to analyze supplier costs. Should-cost modeling is where the buying firm puts together an analysis of the supplier's likely cost of producing a product or service that the buying firm wants to procure. A should-cost model is typically an estimated cost that is created by trying to model the supplier's material costs, labor costs, general and administrative costs, and other overhead costs, along with projected profit margins. This is useful for preparing for a negotiation with suppliers or completing a make-or-buy analysis.

When developing a should-cost model to determine supplier costs and margins, the analyst should try to capture cost drivers and not only the cost elements. For example, what is driving the supplier's labor costs? Why is its direct material 10 percent less costly than another potential supplier? A should-cost model should capture drivers of costs such as labor productivity and wage rates. Capturing drivers produces models that give the analyst much more insight into how and why the supplier is proposing specific prices. Should-cost models that are based on realistic cost drivers provide far more insight for making decisions. Differences in relative sizes of cost components indicate that different ones will dominate each different supplier should-cost model.

Futures and Options

Futures and options are tools that supply chain managers generally use sparingly. Nonetheless, they are important concepts required to understand investment behaviors.

Futures are an agreement between firms to buy or sell a commodity or a financial instrument at a set price on a specific future date. Futures are an obligation to buy the resource, so when a person or firm buys a future, they are committing to the purchase of that commodity and must take possession of the item on the specified date. If the buyer decides that the product will not be needed, the future must be sold to another party interested in buying that commodity on that date. Futures can be included in transportation or other purchase contracts.

An option is the right, but not the obligation, to buy or sell a given stock, stock index, or commodity at a given price on or before a given date. If the buyer decides that the option is no longer needed, the buyer can sell the option to another firm, or let the option expire without using it.

Options consist of two primary types: *puts* and *calls*. An option to sell a stock in the future is called a *put* option, and the right to buy a stock is a *call* option. A call option allows the purchaser to buy the stock at the specified price, which is called the *strike price*. This helps an investor or portfolio manager guarantee that the stock will be able to be bought at a favorable price. Between the time that the option is purchased and the exercise date, the market price may rise above the strike price, in which case the option will be exercised (because the investor can buy the stock more cheaply than the market price and immediately sell it at a profit), or fall below the strike price, in which case the option will not be exercised. In either case, the option allows the manager to reduce the uncertainty of future returns. If the option may be exercised at any time prior to the exercise date, it is known as an *American option*, and if it may only be exercised on the specified date, it is known as a *European option*.

Part of the reason that stock options have become so popular with investors is because they allow an investor to protect against possible large losses due to falls in the price of a stock. If investors buy a stock at

$40 believing that it will appreciate in value but concerned that there is some chance it will go down, they can also purchase a put option to sell the same stock in the future for $40. If the stock falls, the investors will be able to sell the stock for a small loss that comes from buying the put option. The more volatile the stock is, the more likely its price is to vary between the current date and the strike date, and therefore, the greater the chance that the stock will fall below $40 by the strike date. Therefore, greater variability would also mean the investor would have to pay a higher premium for the $40 put option. If the stock goes up to $50, the investor can sell the stock for a profit. If it falls to $30, the investor will sell it for $40, and the only expense to the investor was the cost of the option. However, in this example, the investor did have the original $40 per share tied up in the purchased stock for the whole period of time. Alternatively, if the stock is at $40 and the investor believes the stock will go up, the investor could decide to not buy any stock, and instead buy a call option to buy the stock in the future at $40. If the stock does go up to $50, the investor will buy the stock for $40 and immediately sell it for $50, making a significant profit. If the stock goes down, the investor has only lost the price of the option, and no capital was tied up in owning the stock.

These examples show why options are so popular with investors. They allow firms to manage risk, and guarantee access to a stock at the desired price. They also allow a firm guaranteed access to an asset at a set price that will not rise. The firm does not need to own the asset but can control it.

Futures and Options Trading

Since 1883, grain futures have been traded in the United States.[1] Traders have used futures to manage risk, for speculation reasons, and to control assets without having to invest the entire amount of the cost of the asset. Over time, futures for many other commodities have been created. Futures are now also actively traded for coffee, orange juice, livestock, metals,

---

[1] Morgan, D. (1979). *Merchants of Grain*, No. 338.1731 M6.

petroleum products, currencies, stock market indices, and many other items.

Options trading is a more recent phenomenon. Stock options have been widely traded since 1973 when the Chicago Board of Trade began organized trading in stock options for a few large companies.[2] This was made possible by the acceptance of the work of Fischer Black and Merton Scholes, who provided a theoretically sound method for pricing stock options. Prior to this, trading in stock options was done on a more limited basis because options holders did not have the ability to resell the options before they expired. Since that limited beginning, many more stock options continue to be actively traded with their prices listed in newspapers like *The Wall Street Journal.* The Chicago Board of Options and Exchange (CBOE) offers options on more than 1,500 different equities. The possibility of options trading led to the formation of important companies in the agricultural industry, such as Cargill. The major benefit of trading companies is that they would ensure a farmer a fixed price, providing them with certainty of income, while maximizing their profitability once they sold the crop at the end of the season.

Not all efforts to set up futures trading systems have succeeded. In 2000, Enron attempted to create an internet bandwidth trading exchange.[3] In 2001, Enron announced plans to trade memory chip futures, optimistic that it would succeed where previous efforts to do the same had failed.[4] Ultimately, neither was successful. Bandwidth trading was significantly hurt because supply of bandwidth by far exceeded the demand.[5] Memory chip futures were hampered by the company's financial troubles and the fact that memory chips were not as much of a commodity as Enron had hoped.

---

[2] Chicago Board Options Exchange, History of the CBOE. Retrieved from https://www. cboe.com/aboutcboe/history.

[3] Kirkpatrick, D. (2000). "Enron Takes Its Pipeline to the Net." *Fortune* 141(2), 127–129.

[4] Ojo, B. (2001). "Will DRAM 'Futures' Trading Work this Time? Houston Firm Thinks So." *EBN*, June 18.

[5] Sechler, B. (2001). "Enron Strives to Make a Market in Trading Memory-Chip Futures." *Wall Street Journal*, June 8, p. B5.

Tax-Efficient Supply Chains

Supply chains typically operate in multiple countries and therefore are subject to taxation by multiple jurisdictions. Raw materials and components are sourced in multiple countries and then combined in perhaps another region. Senior management often makes sourcing, production, and distribution decisions based on which locations are most tax efficient. Sometimes these efforts to be tax efficient are called *tax engineering*. Supply chains can be designed in such a way that they minimize the tax due over the course of the movement and manufacturing of the product from origin to destination. Broadly, taxes would fall under the following categories:

1. income taxes levied on corporations,
2. sales taxes (or alternatives such as value-added taxes, VAT, or gross receipt taxes, GRT),
3. excise or use taxes,
4. tariffs.

Income taxes are generally levied on the profit of a firm. Sales taxes, as well as VAT and GRT, are generally regarded as consumption taxes, which are ultimately paid by the consumers. The differences between the three types are that sales tax is charged at the point of sale to the end consumer, while VAT is charged at all levels of the supply chain on the "value-added," and the GRT is levied on all revenues of a firm. Excise and use taxes are charged on a narrow range of products, such as tobacco and alcohol, or vehicles, respectively. Tariffs are charged on imported goods to a country.[6]

The goal of a tax-efficient supply chain is to legally maximize the after-tax profit for the company. This can be achieved by a number of methods, which can include routing shipments through certain tax

---

[6]For a more thorough review of the different taxes, please refer to guides such as the following publication by Earnst and Young, www.ey.com/Publication/vwLUAssets/ey-2017-2018-tp-reference-guide/$FILE/ey-2017-2018-tp-reference-guide.pdf.

jurisdictions, transfer pricing arrangements, royalties, and other tactics. Inside the United States, companies choose certain states to locate in for their favorable tax treatment. An example would be a company locating its West Coast distribution center in the Reno, Nevada area, where there is no state income tax. Compared to neighboring California, where the state corporate tax rate is up to 8.84 percent, Nevada appears very attractive as a place to locate physical and/or financial operations. Several states (Arkansas, Kentucky, Louisiana, Mississippi, Oklahoma, Texas, and West Virginia) tax inventories, which has an impact on warehouses located in these localities.

Internationally, things can get even more complicated. A famous example is the double Irish–Dutch sandwich, which is used by a number of large technology companies. A US company sells its goods in Germany, but the financial transactions involve two Irish companies, one Dutch company, and another in a tax haven country. The home company sells the product via its subsidiary in Ireland, which holds the intellectual property. Taxes due in Ireland are 10–12.5 percent, but the Irish company pays a royalty to a Dutch subsidiary, for which it gets an Irish tax deduction. Royalties are not taxed in the Netherlands. The Dutch company pays for the intellectual property to another subsidiary in Ireland, with no with-holding tax on inter-EU transactions. The second subsidiary, although it is an Irish corporation, pays no corporate income tax because its directors are non-residents. The company is controlled from outside Ireland, in Bermuda, or another so-called "tax haven." Proceeds are then collected in the tax haven, from where it can be used for other global investments.[7] We should note that while these practices have received a lot of attention, there are currently no laws or regulations restricting them.[8] As recently as

---

[7]For a thorough review of this topic, please refer to the article by Farok, J. C. (2017). "Tax Avoidance by Multinational Companies: Methods, Policies, and Ethics." *Rutgers Business Review*, 1(1), 27–43. Retrieved from https://docs.wixstatic.com/ugd/ddcf9a_4a86298550e 64a8bb01325def11c63d4.pdf.

[8]Charles, D. and Kocieniewskil, D. (2012). "How Apple Sidesteps Billions in Taxes." *The New York Times*, April 28, 2012. Retrieved from https://www.nytimes.com/2012/04/29/ business/apples-tax-strategy-aims-at-low-tax-states-and-nations.html.

2017, there are reports that Google used a Dutch shell company in Bermuda to minimize taxes.[9]

Tariffs

Ever since the end of World War II, different institutions have been created to ease the flow of goods between countries. In 1946, the General Agreement on Tariffs and Trade (GATT) was established in addition to other multilateral institutions devoted to international economic cooperation, such as the World Bank and the International Monetary Fund. In 1995, the World Trade Organization (WTO) was established under the umbrella of the prior agreements, which is the organization still governing international trade. The main goal of the WTO is to reduce barriers to trade between countries. Companies navigating the international supply chain benefit from the free movement of goods and services.

However, because tariffs do exist, companies have to circumvent or deal with tariffs. Tariffs are taxes on products that are imported into a specific country. Countries often place tariffs on commodities they wish to protect. One example is the country of origin labeling rules. While a Louis Vuitton handbag may carry a "Made in France" label, the bags are mostly produced in Romania. After assembly, the goods are exported to France, where they are "finished" so that they qualify for a "Made in France" label in accordance with EU law.[10]

In 2018, the United States ramped up tariffs on imports from China that ended up costing American consumers approximately $1.4 billion. These tariffs introduced a great deal of uncertainty in the global trading system as the United States began to introduce several new tariffs on its trading partners. This unilateral action caused trading partners to react,

---

[9]*The Guardian.* "Google Shifted $23 billion to Tax haven Bermuda in 2017, Filing Shows." Retrieved from www.theguardian.com/technology/2019/jan/03/google-tax-haven-bermuda-netherlands.

[10]Lembke, A. (2017). "Revealed: The Romanian Site Where Louis Vuitton Makes Its Italian Shoes." *The Guardian*, June 17, Saturday 04.00 EDT. Retrieved from https://www.theguardian.com/business/2017/jun/17/revealed-the-romanian-site-where-louis-vuitton-makes-its-italian-shoes.

and tariffs in several countries were escalated. For one US automobile manufacturer, the tariffs on shipping vehicles to China went from 15 percent to 25 percent and then finally to 45 percent in the space of one month during the summer of 2018. Global companies do not like uncertainty and, as in the case of Harley-Davidson, which is moving European manufacturing to Europe out of the United States, began to adjust their manufacturing and distribution models to minimize tariffs. Many supply chain executives view tariff avoidance as an important part of their portfolio. Another example is ON Semiconductor, which was able to mitigate the costs of tariffs in 2018. Without this mitigation maneuver of moving production out of China to other locations, it would have had to pay $75 million in tariffs on goods from China. Because it was able to move production, it reduced its tariff expenses to $25 million.

Another example of tax- and tariff-efficient supply management is *completely knocked down production* (CKD). For example, an automobile company can ship all the parts of a car to the destination country and then assemble them locally. In Malaysia, an importer could pay between 30 percent and 100 percent in excise taxes, in addition to customs duties and value-added taxes. CKD can eliminate excise taxes while adding additional costs to assemble the vehicle locally. In the United States, the so-called "Chicken Tax" adds a 25 percent tariff to all light trucks that are imported to the United States. Daimler AG manufactured cargo van versions its Sprinter models in CKD kit form in Düsseldorf, Germany from 2001 to 2006, then shipped to its factory in Gaffney, South Carolina for final assembly, thus avoiding the Chicken Tax. In a more recent example, Tesla operates an assembly plant in Tilburg, Netherlands. It is used for its cars and SUVs for the European Union, which imposed a 10 percent import duty on imported cars. Other European countries that are not part of the EU, such as Norway, receive completed cars shipped directly from the United States. This example is not true CKD production, because the car is still mainly manufactured in the Tesla Factory in Fremont, California. However, during final assembly various parts are added to the car, most notably the rear subframe with the drivetrain in addition to the battery pack. This is likely the minimum amount of work that is necessary to consider the imported components as "parts" and not a complete vehicle.

Cash Conversion Cycle

This section details an important financial metric that is impacted by supply chain managers: the cash conversion cycle (CCC). The CCC connects the firm to the supply chain. It is a meaningful measure, especially for firms that have physical goods. Its application is not just for finance and treasury executives; it also impacts the supply chain domain. The CCC is directly related to the working capital needs of the firm. This direct link is often used by analysts to evaluate the ability of the firm to efficiently manage cash.

Fundamentally, CCC measures the time between the outflow of cash and the inflow of cash directly associated with operating the business. In other words, a lower value for CCC is better than a higher value. Intuitively, a lower cycle time is preferred when converting work into cash. At the firm level, the CCC can be calculated utilizing publicly available information. The information can be found on a firm's income statement and balance sheet, with the necessary components needed for calculation itemized in Table 1. The CCC can be calculated on a quarterly or annual basis.

The importance of the CCC lies in the continuous measurement over time. If a firm can lower its CCC by improving its working capital, then it has freed resources that can be directed to other needs. Often, financial analysts use this metric to gauge the liquidity of a firm.

All three components of the cash conversion cycle can be within the control of the firm's supply chain organization. These elements represent

Table 1: Cash Conversion Cycle

Metric	Description	Calculation
Cash Conversion Cycle (CCC)	A metric describing how efficiently the firm can generate cash.	$CCC = DSO + DIO - DPO$
Days Sales Outstanding (DSO)	The number of days needed to collect on sales.	$DSO = $ Accounts Receivable/Daily Sales
Days Inventory Outstanding (DIO)	How many days it takes to sell the available inventory.	$DIO = $ Inventory/Daily COGS
Days Payable Outstanding (DPO)	The company's payment of its own bills.	$DPO = $ Accounts Payable/Daily COGS

the largest untapped opportunity for the supply chain to fund the organization. Efforts in improving the CCC can have an instant payback — and are more than self-funding. To measure — and ultimately improve — the CCC and its three components, firms must also similarly measure and monitor the fundamental elements that feed into those components, namely aging of inventory, accounts payable, and accounts receivable. Projections for each component should be developed for future periods.[11] Much of the improvement of the cash conversion cycle is derived when the supply chain organization builds a model to project or forecast CCC elements over a rolling forward 12-month basis.

Measuring CCC consistently is a good practice, and it helps check the direction of the firm. There are Wall Street analysts that utilize CCC and its days of inventory (DIO) component to determine whether or not a company is a good investment. For example, some analysts use changes in DIO to determine overall health of the firm. If a firm shows an increase in DIO of 20 percent or more, that is interpreted as a signal for a potential problem within the firm and its supply chain management.

Revenue Generation within the Supply Chain Organization

Often, beyond their normal assigned tasks of managing costs, supply chain organizations are tasked with being revenue generators and not just cost managers. In a recent meeting of chief procurement officers from several universities, many who had spent their lives working in procurement were surprised to find out that they were being asked to capture revenue through rebates and other methods. For many CPOs, this change in expectations has caused a significant shift in their perspectives: They are now being tasked to better integrate upstream procurement with downstream demand management and ultimately contribute to the whole business.

This expanding area of responsibility of revenue capture is still a relatively new concept and not widespread in most supply chain organizations, but it is likely that we will see movement within firms to task their

---

[11] Interview with Gray Williams, September 11, 2018.

supply chain people to also work on generating revenue. This is clearly part of "funding the organization," which is a goal of supply chain financing. While supply chain organizations traditionally have focused on the cost and continuity of supply, now they are being asked to expand those responsibilities and be part of a firm's effort to generate revenue. A portion of the supply chain organization's financial responsibilities are derived from making working capital more efficient as is addressed in a firm's measurement of its cash conversion cycle.

Within a supply chain organization, revenue capture can be achieved through delivering very short and responsive product availability. Some readers will remember the "quick response" programs that many logistics managers utilized beginning in the 1990s. These quick responses focused on shortening lead times and other cycle times to become shorter and more predictable with less variation. These shorter cycle times can be coupled with a tailored inventory strategy to provide lower-cost inventory that is available when it is needed. Walmart's go-to-market strategy reflects this idea. While it wants to be "always the low-price" provider, it really wants to avoid stockouts during the limited hours that shoppers want to visit a Walmart store after work or on the weekends. Competitively advantaged operational cycle times that are short and predictable, coupled with a tailored inventory strategy, can help the firm respond to the market faster and generate revenue (see Table 2).

Economic Value Added

One of the best predictors of a firm's stock price has been changes in its economic value added (EVA). EVA was trademarked by the consulting firm Stern Stewart & Co. EVA "creates clarity so that all the pluses and minuses of these IT decisions can be considered in ways that companies [that don't use EVA] find difficult to do," said Bennett Stewart, co-founder of Stern Stewart & Co. EVA began being used by successful firms, such as GE and Coca-Cola, in the 1980s. Alfred Rappaport, in his book *Creating Shareholder Value: A Guide for Managers and Investors,*[12]

---

[12]Rappaport, A. (1998). *Creating Shareholder Value: A Guide for Managers and Investors* (Rev. and updated), Free Press, New York.

Table 2:   Examples of Revenue Capture within Selected Industries

Industry	Revenue Capture
Consumer Packaged Goods/Consumer Electronics	Keep omni-channel fill rates higher for your products at retailers, distributors, or online. The corollary is also true. If the supply chain organization cannot keep retailer shelves filled or online fill rates competitive, it's likely the retailer will fill the pegs or deliver the online orders with competitive products.
Semiconductors	Supply chain organization can determine when large quarterly allocations of commodity-like memory and microprocessors to OEMs may not come to fruition, and then quickly deliver available end-of-quarter supply to opportunistic buyers, by "selling out" the factory at the highest price.
Aerospace	Supply chain organization develops an inventory strategy that mitigates the impact of 60-week lead time components and cumulative manufacturing lead times of 24 months to deliver a product such as satellite subsystems within 12 months.
Telecom/Datacom	The supply chain organization can enable the firm to offer the shortest availability of optical switches, transceivers, laser assemblies, and other optical components to customers like Cisco, Huawei, Google, or Facebook — that's going to result in more revenue for a company than would normally occur.

described the EVA measurement without referring to it as EVA. EVA moves a supply chain manager's focus on whether or not a project, product, or other investment that will generate returns for the company above the cost of capital and increase value of the firm. Many firms that embrace EVA actually have bonus and compensation plans in place that reward or punish managers for adding value to or subtracting value from the company. The late Roberto Goizueta, legendary former CEO of Coca-Cola during the 1980s and 1990s, said "When I played golf regularly, my average score was 90, so every hole was par 5. I look at EVA like I look at breaking par. At Coca-Cola we were under par and adding a lot of value."[13]

As a measurement, EVA reflects the value of a firm's economic activity above the capital cost of the investment. It is wealth that is returned to

[13]Tully, S. (1993). "The Real Key to Creating Wealth." *Fortune*, 128(6), 38–44.

the firm above and beyond the cost of the capital used to finance the project or products in question. It combines the two primary financial statements: the income statement and the balance sheet. To calculate EVA, the change in economic profit (EP) over time is computed. To obtain EP, the net operating profit after taxes (NOPAT) is developed and a capital charge (the capital investment multiplied by the cost of capital) is subtracted. The formulas for EP and EVA are as follows:

$$EP = NOPAT - \text{capital charge,}$$

where

$$NOPAT = \text{net operating profit after taxes}$$

and

$$\text{capital charge} = (\text{capital investment}) \times (\text{cost of capital}),$$

$$EVA = \Delta EP_{n1,n2}.$$

But, for example, there might not be net operating profit after taxes (NOPAT) arising out of a supply chain investment such as a distribution center, so the net financial benefits of the distribution center investment can be used as a replacement for NOPAT. Consider, for instance, a case where the cost–benefit analysis reveals that a $500,000 investment in a new distribution center will return $80,000 in net quantifiable benefits. The ROI is 16 percent ($80,000 divided by $500,000). The cost of capital in the company is 12 percent. Using the formula above, the EVA in this case is $20,000:

$$\$80,000 \text{ net benefits} - (\$500,000 \text{ capital investment}$$
$$\times 12 \text{ percent cost of capital}) = \$20,000 \text{ EVA.}$$

Another way to calculate EVA in this example is to simply deduct the 12 percent cost of capital from the 16 percent ROI, then multiply by the investment:

$$4 \text{ percent} \times \$500,000 = \$20,000 \text{ EVA.}$$

EVA is always expressed as a dollar amount. This means that the investment must return a profit above the capital cost of the investment. So, EVA prevents managers from thinking that the cost of capital is free. The use of this measurement often moves management to reduce its asset base and outsource more firm functions.

EVA can help managers to use both the balance sheet and the income statement to get a clearer picture of the impact of investments on the business, and additionally, on the market cap of the firm. Everything else being equal, EVA encourages the firm to shed assets. One of the drivers for the push to outsource has been the impact of the EVA measurement on firms. To make the EVA calculation positive, firms reduce the amount of capital they have tied up in operations and increase business activities such as outsourcing. In the logistics sector, outsourcing distribution and manufacturing has come as a result of trying to improve EVA, ROI, and return on assets (ROA). These metrics can be improved by either increasing profitability — the "return" — or decreasing assets and investment.

For example, if a company invests in manufacturing equipment or in a warehouse, how much additional profit will be required to pay for that equipment or facility? Most managers are intuitively aware of the importance of value creation to their businesses, and EVA can help them to quantify that intuition. EVA is a management philosophy and performance measurement that adjusts those goals from mere intuition to a rigorous analysis. It can help ensure that no investment escapes scrutiny.

A fundamental proposition of EVA is that capital has a measurable value and should be factored into every breakeven analysis or ROI model when any investment in a plant, equipment, or a new supply chain management system is considered. EVA stresses the importance that capital — the most carefully managed asset in the majority of firms — not be treated as free, as it typically never is.

Investors tend to like to invest in firms that are "asset-light," which means that they do not have many physical assets. A lower amount of assets makes the ROA and ROI calculations more positive. International logistics firms, freight brokers such as APL Logistics, have few assets and as such investors find them preferable often to "asset-heavy" firms.

Gross Margin Return on Investment

Gross margin return on investment (GMROI) is a metric that is often used in retail businesses but can be applied to other types of firms as well. It is not limited to retail. It is a measurement that explains how many gross margin dollars are earned on every dollar of inventory investment. GMROI combines the effects of profits and inventory turnover. It works almost like a hurdle rate to determine whether or not the investment in a specific product is producing profit. GMROI calculation can be used to measure the performance of the entire shop, but it is more effective if used for a particular department or category of merchandise. The formula is as follows:

$$\text{GMROI} = \text{gross margin/average inventory.}$$

If it is not possible to calculate average inventory, ending inventory level can be utilized instead. The result is a ratio indicating the number of times gross margin is earned from the inventory investment. In many cases this metric is used to determine which products and product lines should be discontinued.

Definition of Tobin's Q Ratio

Tobin's Q or the Q ratio is the ratio of the market value of a company's assets as measured by the market value of its outstanding stock and debt divided by the replacement cost of the company's assets at their book value. It evaluates the ratio of the market value of a firm to the replacement cost of its assets.[14] The method of calculating a Q ratio is described below as follows:

$$Q \text{ ratio} = \frac{\text{total market value of firm} + \text{liabilities}}{\text{total asset (book) value} + \text{liabilities}}.$$

---

[14]Tan, K., Kannan, V. R., Handfield, R. B. and Ghosh, S. (1999). "Supply Chain Management: An Empirical Study of Its Impact on Performance." *International Journal of Operations & Production Management*, 19(10), 1034–1052. Retrieved from https://doi.org/10.1108/01443579910287064.

Q ratios can also be used for calculating a stock market valuation. In this case the aggregate of the stock market values for companies in a given stock market or index is divided by the aggregate of the replacement value of the firm's assets. In September 2013, a *Financial Times* columnist examined two competing ways of analyzing stock market valuations — the *Q* ratio and Cape.[15] Although the two methods used very different calculations, both pointed to the fact that the US stock market was significantly overvalued leading some to question the accuracy of both methods.

---

[15]Authers, J. (2013). "Measuring the Gauges of US Stock Valuations." *Financial Times*, September 1.

Chapter 4

Funding Growth through Supply Chain Improvements

Introduction

To expand into new markets, fund research and development, or execute any activity that requires investment, firms need access to capital. However, accessing capital is not easy and it remains a critical issue for firms. Credit markets in the United States have improved considerably since the worst periods in early 2009, but it still is often difficult for a firm to obtain access to credit. Outside the United States, in countries such as Brazil, financial flows have dramatically worsened.

How can firms use their supply chains to improve the funding of the firm? In this chapter, we discuss the importance of the supply chain in obtaining operating capital and offer a few examples of leading firms that use their supply chains to fund growth. We conclude with strategies of how supply chain organizations can obtain working capital for the firm. Finally, an example is presented depicting how firms can strengthen their supply bases and help small- or medium-sized suppliers with their capital needs and business acumen.

As mentioned, there are limited sources of funds available to firms. Despite general easing in credit markets, many non-investment-grade companies and small or medium enterprises (SMEs) continue to find it difficult to finance their working capital requirements. As shown in

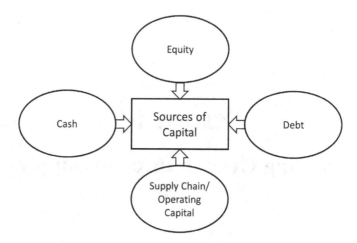

Figure 1:   Sources of Capital

Figure 1, there are four primary sources of capital within the firm. These sources are debt, equity, supply chain (often referred to as operating capital or retained earnings), and cash. Of these, cash is the most liquid, but depending on the business model of the firm it can be the most difficult to acquire. Equity capital is generally the most expensive. Currently, debt capital is relatively cheap, but it is a limited resource. Companies can only borrow a limited amount.

The least expensive and easiest capital to accumulate is supply chain/ operating capital. Operating capital is accumulated by reducing the cost of supply chain processes and utilizing the supply chain to increase revenues. Operating capital does not need to be "applied for" with a bank or Board of Directors, and it can quickly be turned into cash that can be used elsewhere in the firm.

Operating Capital in the Supply Chain

The Basel III restrictions, introduced in 2010 and phased in over the following five years, require banks to create capital buffers that impact bank capital requirements by holding them responsible to increase liquidity and reduce their leverage. Consequently, Basel III has forced many small banks to cut back on loans to businesses.[1] These changes, in addition to a general climate in the financial industry moving toward conservative capital management, have forced companies to figure out how to find alternative methods of self-funding their growth.

Equity markets have not seen much growth in several industry sectors. For example, products from some consumer packaged goods companies have been selling well around the world, but their stock value — and subsequently the value of the firms — has not grown much over the last several years. Therefore, investors have not funded these firms to the level at which they need to grow in accordance with investor expectations. Firms cannot issue much more equity because it would dilute their stock holdings, which is generally not preferable.

There is a significant credit arbitrage between large companies and their suppliers. Supply chain financing programs that allow for reverse factoring, one of which is described later in this book, can assist buyers to monetize this arbitrage, while at the same time improving operations for their suppliers.

Developing Operating Capital

As mentioned, the best capital for a firm, other than pure cash, is operating capital. An important point of departure from what we have known about supply chain management begins with an observation that a large percentage of a firm's operating capital is embedded in the supply chain.

This observation can help redefine the role of supply managers who are tasked with cutting operational costs. These savings fund operating capital and enable the firm to make investments in new products or services and also in new markets that could not necessarily support themselves without access to capital. An important job for supply chain managers is to look for various ways to free up operating capital that can be immediately applied to new and important internal investments.

---

[1] McGrane, V. (2012). "Small Banks are Blunt in Dislike of New Rules." *The Wall Street Journal*. Retrieved from www.wsj.com/articles/SB100008723963904435455045775633 52622533704.

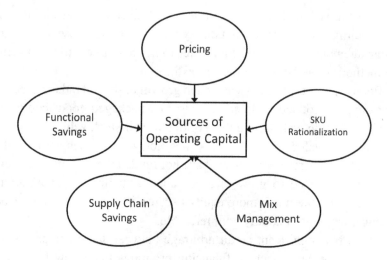

Figure 2:   Sources of Operating Capital

A large food and beverage company interviewed for this research serves as a benchmark in this regard. It has a formalized program to develop operating capital, which is shown in Figure 2. This company is both a manufacturer and retailer, working with a complex mix of different supply chains. Its formalized program uses five main sources to develop operating capital.

Pricing

A firm that has flexibility in its pricing may have the ability to attach a premium price to some of its products. Those products that have price inelasticity can be used to help fund new products and markets that cannot yet support themselves. For example, a cup of coffee from a well-known brand such as Starbucks has pricing flexibility. While it is unlikely that Starbucks could charge $30 for one cup of coffee, it is a product for which prices can be increased based on firm objectives and not entirely based on a capricious marketplace.

SKU Rationalization

Another source of operating capital is obtained through rationalizing SKUs. Firms, like the food and beverage manufacturer mentioned above, carry a fair amount of new products and tend to end up with a proliferation of products that are not top performers. This company maintains a structured program to eliminate SKUs that are lagging. The savings from eliminating products that have not performed well are diverted to new products that can enable company growth.

Mix Management

A mix management strategy is where the firm carefully manages all the elements of the marketing mix to help customers select higher margin offerings. This can include convincing the customer to trade up to a more profitable product or service. Products and services can be bundled together differently so that the cost of purchasing and selling those products and their components can be optimized. This is another way of developing operating capital. A firm can carefully examine its sets of products moving through various supply chains to determine how to manage the mix of those items. At least one firm interviewed realized substantial savings with this type of program.

Supply Chain Savings

Purchasing raw materials and components at lower prices and rationalizing the number and location of plants and warehouses are some ways to find supply chain savings. For many firms, this category of operating capital is likely the most accessible for finding savings. Again, achieving supply chain savings is an important method for funding the firm, and sometimes for funding other members of the supply chain. This category may include changing supply chain intermediaries or reducing the costs related to suppliers and intermediaries. It is typically already part of a firm's supply planning.

Functional Savings

Functional savings refer to transforming a function inside the firm to be more cost efficient. Quite often, this effort translates into rationalizing the personnel that the firm has working in a specific area. It might include cutting part of a function or realigning a business unit to simplify organizational structure. Functional savings usually remain internal to the firm, while supply chain savings are typically external. At one company interviewed, functional savings has included rationalizing each portion of the organization. This company frequently performs a check on operations to determine whether each part of the organization is necessary. If it is discovered that an area is inefficient, there is a readjustment made to bring costs inline.

Fund the Growth

One consumer packaged goods company has a supply chain financing organization that looks to both the finance and supply chain management organizations. With its "Fund the Growth" initiative, the supply chain financing group strives to manage working capital to invest in growth opportunities for the firm. Its primary mission is to fund the growth of the company by transforming its supply chains to be more efficient. Globally, this firm has been successful in consistently increasing gross margins, while at the same time reducing costs, which enables the company to fund new growth such as new product development and marketing programs. Such new initiatives, in turn, produce profit.

Supplier Relationship Building through SCF

An innovative healthcare firm uses SCF techniques to develop suppliers while improving its working capital and cash flow. This firm works with a number of relatively small, privately held suppliers that need help with financing and business acumen. These suppliers may have an important technology that, if properly developed, could be a high-growth product line for this healthcare firm. Through supply chain financing, a small but entrepreneurial supplier can tap into the larger and more established buying firm's strong, blue-chip balance sheet (i.e., credit rating). SCF helps the supplier do a much better job in managing its business. For this healthcare firm, this is part of its supplier relationship management practices, in particular supplier development.

As part of this supplier development initiative, the healthcare firm began identifying a list of suppliers that fit the criteria of having unique technology or a product line that could potentially grow into a large business for the firm. The identified suppliers were typically smaller, privately held companies with revenues in the $100–300 million range. The firm takes advantage of its strong balance sheet and business acumen to help the suppliers' financial back-end processes so that they can then reinvest in their businesses.

In this example, the healthcare firm as a buyer is supporting the supply chain. In return, the buying firm is able to purchase something that it does not have the internal capability to produce. The supplier perhaps does not excel at some aspects of the business operation because it is less experienced and under-financed. Using the buying firm's balance sheet and business understanding helps the supplier to be healthier.

Even for larger suppliers with a similar credit rating, SCF practices are put in place to control cash flow. These processes allow the suppliers to be able to get cash in a timely fashion and to manage their cash flow. More importantly, the buying firm understands that it is strong in the marketplace if its suppliers are strong. In the case company, these programs are tied to its long-term relationship and engagement activities with suppliers so that everyone wins. In this regard, helping suppliers with cash flow and improving their business processes takes on strategic importance. It is an example of one side of the definition of supply chain financing: *Using the organization to fund the supply chain.*

A large part of supplier relationship management for those types of suppliers discussed above is for the buying firm to think through its long-term strategy. The consideration should include the financing component. In this example, the buying firm is saying to the supplier, "We want you to grow with us on a global basis and we can help you figure out how to scale up." From a cost standpoint, at the time of the interview, this particular healthcare firm was transitioning this category of suppliers into the electronic payment process and consolidating them into one vendor payment process. This translates into savings in the firm's accounts payable process by paying through one process instead of multiple processes.

For the suppliers, they get an attractive source of liquidity. By using SCF and/or dynamic discounting (see Chapter 6), the supplier can take the cash at the time of its choice. It can choose the option to take the payment early or wait for the full term to collect the cash. If it elects to take the early payment option, the discount can be based on the buyer's credit profile. As a result, the supplier gains the flexibility of when to collect the payments. Its cash flow improves by reducing its accounts receivables and obtaining cash. In addition, it can improve its balance sheet debt/equity ratio because it has less financial liability to its bank. It also enhances payment transparency because now the supplier has visibility into and control of when the payment is being made. Overall, the supplier is able to predict its cash flow better and control the cash management for its business.

Chapter 5

Methods of Payment

Introduction

How does the money move behind a supply chain? In this chapter, we provide an overview of how financial transactions are routed in the financial system. These routes are an integral part of how SCF is transacted and influences the firms involved. Beginning with traditional paper-based checks, we review commercial credit cards and other electronic bank payment methods, such as automated clearinghouse (ACH) and wire transfers.

It should be noted that the least expensive method for sending a payment is usually ACH, followed by checks, and wire transfers; the most expensive option is a card payment. All methods of payment described in this chapter have certain advantages, and we pay special attention to commercial cards, as there are a number of innovations in this space.

Checks

While checks are still being used by some firms, their popularity is overall on the decline. The Federal Reserve estimates that the use of checks in business-to-business (B2B) transactions declined by 9.2 percent per year for the period 2009–2012 and by 5.5 percent per year in the seven years prior to that.[1] It is interesting to note that in more recent years, the decline has slowed, suggesting certain barriers.

Many firms continue to cling to the mailing and processing of paper checks. Currently, about half of the invoices for US firms are still being paid via check.[2] This is surprising because the cost of writing a check has been estimated to be between \$4 and \$20.[3] One motivation for continuing to use checks may be the working capital benefits that arise from their use. There is typically a delay of several days between the mailing, processing, and posting of checks, which means that the buying firm holds on to its cash longer. However, the administrative burden can be excessive and therefore we see this form of payment eventually losing its standing.

Commercial Cards

Currently, procurement is where the growth of commercial cards is coming from. A key characteristic of the procurement card is that its use tends to be more resistant to recession than travel cards, because travel is viewed as less critical to the operation of the business and therefore is more likely to be restricted in an economic downturn. This has not gone unnoticed in the commercial card industry. The major drivers for the use of commercial cards are efficiencies in the transaction, better visibility, and better financial returns obtained through rebates. In addition, some credit card issuers have been able to help firms with working capital improvements by placing those payments on average 45 days after the transaction. North America is by far the most developed market for commercial cards, followed by Europe. Asia and Latin America are rapidly developing a market. According to one executive we spoke with, adoption of commercial cards in Africa has helped reduce corruption there.

Commercial credit cards can simplify the administrative side of payments, especially to small, niche suppliers. In addition, there is advantage

---

[1] Gerdes, G. R. *et al.* (2013). "The 2013 Federal Reserve Payments Study." Retrieved from www.frbservices.org/assets/news/research/2013-fed-res-paymt-study-detailed-rpt.pdf.

[2] Monga, V. (2014). "U.S. Companies Cling to Writing Paper Checks." *The Wall Street Journal*. Retrieved from www.wsj.com/articles/SB1000142405270230473280457942523 3344430424.

[3] *Ibid.*

to accounts payables. The default payment term for commercial cards is typically 45 days and can be extended. The billing cycle typically lasts one month and then the customer receives another month to pay the bill, which should on average equate to a 45-day term. However, the payment term could be significantly longer or shorter depending on the timing of card use. Lastly, there are the benefits of a rebate on the purchases.

We see significant opportunities to strengthen the use of commercial credit card programs. The US federal government has been a proponent of commercial cards. It has developed a program called SmartPay that routes about $30 billion in spending annually onto cards.[4] MasterCard and Visa anchor the program and are joined by these three banks: US Bank, Citigroup, and JPMorgan Chase.

Types of Commercial Credit Cards

When judging commercial credit cards by popularity, most firms use cards for travel. However, other types of commercial cards are gaining popularity. Procurement, or p-cards, are the second most popular category and used by most organizations. The two lesser known categories of cards are ghost cards and virtual cards.

Not an actual plastic card, a ghost card represents a set of numbers that is specific to a company or a specific department within a company. Purchases can be charged back to the department and the costs are easily assigned. It provides employees with easy access. Further, a ghost card can be assigned to selected suppliers, who can then charge the card number when a purchase is made. This reduces the administrative paperwork that is typically associated with each purchase. Most importantly, the data stream on these purchases is granular and provides great control.

Virtual cards have the highest level of security and the largest number of controls. Suppose an organization needs to refuel its private airplanes. When the plane arrives at a particular airport to refuel, the pilot can use a virtual card to pay, rather than cash or regular credit cards. When the pilot calls in, the procurement organization checks for authenticity and then generates a temporary card number. The pilot presents this number to

---

[4]For more information, please see: https://smartpay.gsa.gov/.

the fueling station and his plane is refueled. The card number is restricted for that particular fueling station for whatever the amount is and is valid only for a point in time. The fueling station gets an immediate authorization and validates the transaction. An overview of different types of commercial cards is shown in Table 1.

Commercial Card Transactions

As shown in Table 2, there are three types of firms that are involved in a card transaction. The buyer has a card issued by its bank, which can be on either the Visa or the MasterCard network. On the receiving end of the transaction, there is the merchant acquirer, who is connected to the seller and receives the funds.

A general process for commercial card transactions is outlined in Figure 1. The transaction entails moving the payment from the issuer to the processor (MasterCard or Visa) network and then to the acquirer. As the card is used, the card issuer routes the payment through the transmitter/processor in a process that is referred to as "interchange," to the merchant acquirer who then deposits the payment into the seller's account.

Table 1:   Types of Commercial Credit Cards

Type of Card	Description
Corporate Travel Card	Travel cards are the most popular type of card, intended to manage expense programs for travel and entertainment purposes.
Purchasing Card	The so-called "p-card" is used primarily for lower value purchases and is typically not used with contracts or purchase orders.
Ghost Card	A ghost card is not a credit card made of plastic. It represents randomly generated credit card numbers that can be attached to a particular vendor or linked to a buying organization. The seller initiates payment and there are numerous controls that can be placed on the account.
Virtual Card	The virtual card is similar to a ghost card in that there is no physical card. Account numbers are generated for specific purchases and can be limited to payment amount, range of time, purpose, and supplier. After use, the account number expires. It garners the greatest number of controls on the user.

Table 2:   Types of Firms Involved in Card Transactions

Function	Purpose
Issuer	Financial institution that issues the card to the buyer consolidates the payments at the end of the billing cycle and provides fraud protection. The issuer is typically a bank such as Citibank or Wells Fargo.
Transmitter/ Processor	Owns and operates the network of interchange between the issuer and the acquirer. The transmitter/processor is typically MasterCard or Visa.
Merchant Acquirer	Financial institution (i.e., bank) that has a relationship with the seller and provides the routing of the transaction to the network's processing facilities. The acquirer allows the merchant (i.e., seller) to accept card payment. This institution is typically a different bank than the issuer.

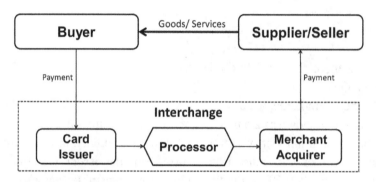

Figure 1:   The Credit Card Transaction Process

This process takes approximately two business days from the submission of the payment to the merchant acquirer's release of the payment to the seller. The buyer pays a consolidated bill 30 days after the end of the billing cycle, which is on average 45 days from the date of the transaction.

Using commercial cards to make a payment entails relatively low administrative overhead. According to the head of commercial credit cards for a large bank, the cost of processing an invoice is around $75, while the cost of processing a purchase order (PO) is around $250. Compare that to the average value of a credit card transaction at $4. This method of payment is attractive, especially for smaller transactions. Through the various intermediaries in the card transaction, there are a number of fees that successively get charged to a vendor. As shown in

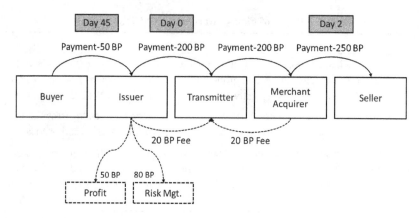

Figure 2:   Credit Card Processing Fees

Note: BP = base points.

Figure 2, there are cascading fees that are charged by each firm in the interchange.

In the example depicted in Figure 2, the total charge associated with the payment is shown as 2.5 percent (or 250 basis points, BP). The fees can vary based on a number of factors that will be explained in Appendix A. Upon receipt of the transaction information, the issuer transmits the payment minus 200 BP to the transmitter. The transmitter passes on that payment to the merchant acquirer without a discount, but both the issuer and the merchant acquirer pay the transmitter a fee of 20 BP. The merchant acquirer then credits the seller's account the payment amount with a total discount of 250 BP. The seller typically receives the deposit within two days after the payment has been initiated. The buyer does not immediately pay the charge but is issued a consolidated bill. This bill can include a discount of 50 BP or more in some cases. The payment typically occurs 30 days after the close of the billing cycle. Since the average transaction can be anywhere from the first to the last day in the billing cycle, on average a transaction is 15 days from the close of each billing cycle. Therefore, on average, firms using a commercial card have a days payable outstanding (DPO) of 45 days on those charges. Furthermore, the issuer does not keep the entire 200 BP discount, but allocates 80 BP to risk management and fraud prevention; the remaining 50 BP are profit.

Table 3: Corporate Card Rebate Example

Annual Spend Volume ($)	Rebate (BP)	Rebate ($)
10,000,000	24	24,000
25,000,000	39	97,500
50,000,000	76	380,000
75,000,000	99	742,500
100,000,000	122	1,220,000
120,000,000	129	1,548,000
140,000,000	135	1,890,000
150,000,000	140	2,100,000
160,000,000	142	2,272,000
170,000,000	143	2,431,000
180,000,000	145	2,610,000
190,000,000	148	2,812,000
200,000,000	149	2,980,000
225,000,000	151	3,397,500

Rebate Structures in Commercial Cards

There are varying rebate fee structures depending on the annual spend volume. These rebates are negotiated between the issuer and the buying firm when a card program is established. Table 3 provides a list of sample rebates that can be achieved on travel accounts. It should be noted that this is the higher end of discount structures, and the typical rebates are usually lower on non-travel accounts.

Some firms have tried to streamline accounts payables, especially for smaller amounts, by implementing policies where they move payments below a certain threshold exclusively onto cards. As previously mentioned, there is a cost advantage for using commercial cards for smaller transactions. There is a breakeven cost for credit card transactions. For example, if we assume that the cost of using a card is 2.5 percent of the transaction value, and the cost of processing an invoice is $75, then at least every transaction below $3,000 should be moved to a card — $75 divided by 2.5 percent is $3,000. If we take into account the existence of a rebate and the A/P advantage, as described previously, firms should move charges of less than $10,000 onto cards. Of course, the final determination of what charges should move to a card depends on the individual firm's characteristics and can vary somewhat.

Electronic Bank Payment Methods (ACH, Wire Transfers)

ACH transactions are electronic forms of payment routed through an automated system that verifies the individual transactions. The service is often free for large customers. It involves centralized external processing (outside of the banks), and transactions are processed in batches. Therefore, it can take a couple of days for transactions to clear.

Wire transfers are typically bank-to-bank transactions. Unlike ACH transactions, wire transfers can be completed quickly, within a few minutes. However, they are much more costly than ACH, costing as much as $50 per transaction. In the United States, wire transfers are routed through the Federal Reserve System. International payments are routed through other networks such as the Society for Worldwide Interbank Financial Telecommunication (SWIFT), the largest international financial communications network linking more than 10,000 financial institutions and other corporations in more than 200 countries.

Chapter 6

Supply Chain Financing Programs

Introduction

How often is procurement performance measured on improvements in working capital or cash flows? Interestingly, not often. The procurement group's key metric is cost reduction, often measured on year-to-year parts price variance (PPV). If the procurement organization does not see the value proposition of the SCF program, it is unlikely it will work in the long run. Firms that want to implement SCF need to make sure the purchasing organization is incentivized in the right way. The procurement organization should be leading the charge to implement SCF, and its activities should be aligned with corporate goals. For instance, a purchasing manager in one organization said, "Why should I go out and extend my payment terms from 30 to 60 days when at the end of the day the only thing that I'm getting measured against is price reduction?"

At the end of the day, success of implementing these SCF programs will hinge on how well the objectives of purchasing organizations are aligned with the organizational objectives. A purchasing organization needs to be incentivized through performance measures that promote SCF. Could the buying company use the speed at which invoices are approved as part of a procurement performance KPI? Paying suppliers on time is one of the most important activities required to build good buyer–supplier relationships. And it is one of the reasons to adopt an SCF program with an external funder, because having the discipline to standardize invoices leads to better relations with the supplier. It is like the old joke: "The check is in the mail." If it is a standardized system, the supplier can depend on when it is getting paid; even reliable payments that occur under relatively lengthy payment terms are easier to manage than payments that are variable, unreliable, and inconsistent.

SCF programs may emerge and gain traction for a company or chain of companies, depending on what factors will motivate the decision-makers. For example, the selling points may be standardizing payment terms (good for the supplier) while improving working capital (good for buyer and/or supplier). In another instance, dynamic discounting (good for the supplier) and better relationships (good for both) might be the key incentives. The messages to the supply chain must clearly explain how this program could be good for both the buyer and the supplier. The project plans for implementing SCF programs typically consist of three work streams — the legal work stream, onboarding, and IT implementation. Systems issues, such as incorrectly transmitted or late payments, can be an inhibitor to these types of programs. Implementing SCF will vary for different firms, whether buying or supplying. Typically, if working with a large bank, SCF implementation can take three to four months.

In this chapter, we will review the types of supply chain financing tools that firms are applying to their supply chains. The entities that are involved include banks, credit card processors, financial technology (fintech) companies, and non-bank funders.

Trade Finance

The key product of the large banks for business customers is trade finance. Often, SCF programs are defined by the banks as part of global trade finance. It is part of financing and commercial lending and includes risk mitigation. Trade finance can also include tools, such as letters of credit. While letters of credit are less utilized for cross-border transactions now, for large ticket items where the parties need to limit risk, letters of credit are still common. For example, an oil tanker being delivered may have a value in excess of $100 million. In that case, a letter of credit that is carefully drafted and executed would be used to guarantee payment. In addition, SCF programs can be used to ensure payment and reduce risk. If a bank has installed an SCF program with a buyer, it will pay the supplier and deduct the approved invoice amount from the buyer's account. The process is automated, as the bank makes sure the payment is processed. This greatly reduces the risk for the supplier of not getting paid by the buying firm.

Because the bank is an intermediary in the transaction, it can make the transaction happen even if the buying firm has a questionable financial status. During the recession in 2009, banks found several suppliers that wanted to join their SCF programs because their buyers were on shaky ground. For example, many automotive suppliers were very concerned about liquidity and saw that some of the OEMs were susceptible to bankruptcy.

Pre-Shipment Finance

Suppliers often borrow from their local market banks and trading companies to fund their working capital. To influence the pricing of the loan, the guiding factor is the supplier's own credit standing. If the supplier is not very well rated or a small private company without easy access to cheap capital, its pricing on the pre-shipment finance program could be high. Pricing may also be impacted by both the supplier's currency and country. While US dollar (USD) SCF pricing could be less than 10 percent, for instance, in a local currency outside the United States it could be higher than 10 percent. Based on geographic and financial risk levels in that country and currency, the price of pre-shipment SCF would vary. When they are engaged in pre-shipment finance activities, some banks may use a purchase order from a well-reputed buyer (e.g., Walmart).

ASN Financing

Advanced Ship Notice (ASN) is something most retailers and manufacturers require their suppliers to submit electronically in advance of a shipment. The ASN is transmitted through the EDI 856 transaction. It communicates the contents of a planned shipment of an order to the customer. A typical ASN includes information about the order, product description, packaging, carrier, etc. The value of this for the customer is that it tells the customer what and when exactly items are going to arrive. The customer can then plan ahead knowing when the shipment will arrive and if everything that was ordered is on the purchase order, or if it is only a partial shipment.

Firms have begun to utilize ASN-based supply chain financing. This relatively new technique allows the supplier to work with a fintech and receive early payment on an invoice once it has transmitted an ASN to the customer. In some cases this can precede the approved invoice.

Post-Shipment Finance

When the buyer accepts an invoice and sponsors the SCF program, it is generally referred to as supply chain finance or reverse factoring because it is not the supplier that is locally factoring the receivable. Post-shipment finance takes place in the same way. In the post-shipment finance program, the price is based on the credit standing of the buyer, as in the case of reverse factoring. For example, a large financially strong buying firm, such as Walmart, would likely have a credit risk around 1 percent per annum. The program is meant to be a benchmark of the buyer's risk of non-payment, which in the case of a firm such as Walmart would not be very high. Other benchmarks to assess buyer risk could be the pricing of its credit default swaps (CDS), commercial paper, corporate bonds, or its revolving credit facility.

In contrast, another form of post-shipment finance can involve the supplier pledging its accounts receivables with a local factor/asset-based finance lender. This program then is factoring rather than reverse factoring. If those receivables are not yet accepted by the buyer, the pricing would likely be higher than a buyer-sponsored post-shipment, post-acceptance SCF agreement. Additionally, suppliers typically do not receive 100 cents on the dollar; the factor may advance around 80–90 percent or in some cases less. Lenders must account for the fact that the buyer has some likelihood of discounting the invoice amount, due to various reasons, such as disputes, discounts, and other charges.

Accounts Receivable and Payable Finance

Accounts receivable finance can also be part of working capital solutions. It can include pooled or single-named programs to fund receivables that might not be eligible for traditional SCF. It can also include foreign and large corporations that are not secured. It can also apply to multi-year contract monetization of licenses, products, royalties, or services.

Accounts payable finance, which is synonymous with supply chain finance and reverse factoring, offers early settlement to suppliers given extended payment terms. It can include a re-invoicing service for the buying company to pay the discount cost in return for more rapid working capital improvement.

Supply Chain Finance

What was previously known as "reverse factoring" is the basis for what most providers call *supply chain finance*, and for this book they are used synonymously. There are several ways a firm can implement a program, but at its core, suppliers receive the option to obtain early payment for a small fee that is calculated based on the buyer's credit risk. Broadly, we have bank-led programs and multi-bank technology platforms.

Background on Supply Chain Finance

For the last 30 years firms have been working to reduce inventories, because with lower inventories they can have more cash, more flexibility, and leaner operations. They also have been working on extending their payment terms. The longer the accounts payable terms are, the better off a firm's working capital will be. To lower their cost of goods sold and/or to extend their payment terms, large firms take advantage of their better credit ratings. In doing so they are able to attract better suppliers that choose to accept these terms in either lower prices or extended payment. Several firms we spoke with consider supply chain finance as a way of building a deeper relationship with their suppliers. In many cases the contracts with suppliers may not have been examined in years. During the process of implementing SCF, the buying firm may find things it didn't realize were actually happening. For instance, suppliers may have multiple subsidiaries that are dealing with multiple subsidiaries of the buyer. These trends have been beneficial for buying firms but have constrained suppliers in some ways. Suppliers with smaller operations may not be able

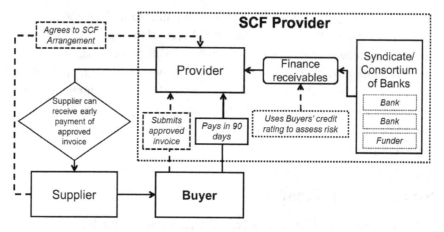

Figure 1:   SCF Transactions

to compensate for drawn-out payments; suppliers may value their own working capital for improvements or development; suppliers may have other immediate cash needs based on their buying practices. To resolve this dilemma, supply chain finance introduces a third party (often a bank) into the mix. This entity absorbs the discrepancy in cash flow, allowing the supplier to be paid in a more timely fashion and the buyer to pay on extended terms. Suppliers "pay" for this service, but reap the benefits of liquidity.

The basic notion of supply chain finance programs is that buyers are able to pay their suppliers at a specified time (e.g., 90 days), while allowing the supplier to receive early payments (e.g., as early as two days after invoice approval). A typical arrangement is shown in Figure 1. Solid lines indicate movement of money or goods, while broken lines reflect facilitating activities, such as agreements. Generally, payments are routed through the provider, which can be a bank or a fintech company. The provider will then manage the relationship with the funders, who often are banks but can also be insurance companies, mutual funds, or retirement funds. It is also the provider who has the direct financing relationship with the supplier. It is important that the buyer is outside the day-to-day decisions of the provider. If the supplier agrees to the arrangement, it receives early payment, at a discounted rate that is based on the buyer's credit. The supplier would basically enjoy short-term liquidity at a favorable rate.

At a casual glance, large banks appear to have much better programs because they have capital, or at least presumably cheaper access to capital. However, several interviewees stated this was the wrong way to think about it. The fintech options are considered "bank-agnostic," where fintech firms act more as brokers using multi-bank platforms. They can approach different banks and get the best solution because one bank may potentially not agree to the terms attractive to the customer. Consider the way 3PLs arrange transportation: It used to be that a firm would have all of its transportation contracted with one trucking company. But a 3PL (e.g., CH Robinson, Ceva, DAMCO, or Exel) is able to pick and choose a transport company in much the same way as a brokerage. In this regard, fintechs operate like 3PLs do. Among the fintech companies, competition takes place mostly around the technology platform and the onboarding of suppliers, rather than the access to capital. It is important to note that multi-bank fintech platforms have increased the cost competition of supply chain finance to the point where profits have been reduced significantly. In comparison, the banks' proprietary systems' have shown more inertia, which makes them slower to change. Firms outside of banks are joining the ranks of funders. For example, insurance companies such as Prudential and MetLife seek to buy short-term debt, and they are often willing to accept a lower return than banks. In some cases, this might be as low as 20 basis points over bond pricing.

Interest Rates Involved in Supply Chain Finance Programs

One of the major benefits of supply chain finance programs is the access to lower interest rates. However, there has been a great deal of discussion recently about interest rates in reverse factoring arrangements. According to our investigation, the typical interest rate for reverse factoring or supply chain financing programs fluctuated for a typical program. That means that companies that are rated at BB should expect 150 BP (1.5 percent APR) over LIBOR, and higher-rated companies should be somewhat lower. For companies that are not rated, the interest rates are higher.

Figure 2:   Historical LIBOR Rates

These rates are expected to change. Figure 2 shows the changes in LIBOR rates over the last 30 years. In September 2018, the US Federal Reserve announced an increase in interest rates. It is important to note that when LIBOR changes, all interest rates change with it, while the spread between the overall APR and LIBOR is typically set to stay constant. However, this should not diminish the attractiveness of these SCF programs. Since suppliers' interest rates are still going to be higher, they will likely find lower-priced capital by joining their customers' SCF programs.

Interest rates vary in a buyer-sponsored program. If a company is rated CCC or worse, its credit risk could be priced at 8 percent or higher. In 2018, a buyer rated BBB or better would typically not be higher than 3–4 percent. Outside of the United States, the interest rate can be much higher. In one example from 2016, a BB-rated company had a 1.5 percent APR reverse factoring rate. The return for the banks lies in their cost of capital. If banks can borrow at close to LIBOR, any returns above that would be accretive, notwithstanding other fixed costs.

Dynamic Discounting

Another technique firms utilize is dynamic discounting. This technique allows the supplier the option to receive direct early payment from the buyer at a variable discount rate. While the buyer cannot rely on outside financing and must set aside a certain amount of cash to disburse, it may receive additional discounts when it pays its suppliers early.

For example, if a firm has a standard 2/10 net 30 term and it chooses to apply the same discount in a dynamic manner, then the daily interest would be 0.1 percent (20 days earlier payment in exchange for 2 percent). Therefore, if a supplier wanted to get paid 30 days early it would be charged a 3 percent discount. The downside of this tool is that the buyer has to use its own money, since it is a direct payment.

Yet another variation is offered by fintech firms. The fintech firm can apply an auction model to dynamic discounting, rather than a fixed discount structure. For example, if a buying firm has a certain amount of cash to disburse to its suppliers in exchange for additional discounts, then it can auction off those early payments. The platform will create a session akin to a reverse auction, where suppliers can bid for that early payment. So, for suppliers who need to accelerate collection of their outstanding receivables, they have the ability to join this auction via the online platform. In contrast, there may be suppliers that do not want the buyer to know they are willing to offer discounts for early payment. For these suppliers, a fintech can conduct a similar reverse auction, except this time it would be drawing money from sources other than the buyer.

Strategies to Manage the Various Tools

A buying firm may want to use the tools we describe in this chapter in a comprehensive fashion. To do that, the overall goal of the program must be established. It may be twofold: accounts payable optimization and early payment discounts. The attractiveness of accounts payable optimization (often called DPO extension) lies in the improvement of working capital. Early payment discounts often go against working capital efficiencies, and rather contribute to the improvement of the firm's cost structure.

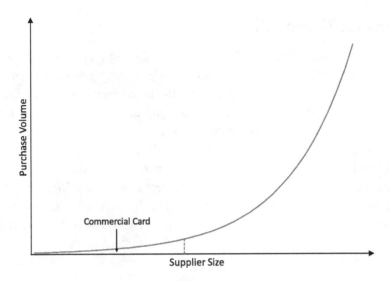

Figure 3:   Targeting of Commercial Card Programs

The first tool that firms should consider is a robust commercial card program. As can be seen in Figure 3, the ideal suppliers for this program are typically smaller suppliers or low-value suppliers of non-critical items. Commercial card programs are desirable because buyers gain savings and can extend payables. The buying firm obtains a rebate, typically in the 50–150 BP range, and gains a DPO of 45 days for those payables. Longer DPO can be achieved at a reduced rebate. Then, what would be the threshold at which the card program strategy will be implemented? That is, what is the largest transaction that will be charged on a card? In some cases, we heard of limits of $2,500, while other companies push the maximum amount beyond that, closer to the large-ticket cutoff where the credit card fees become smaller.

The second tool is dynamic discounting. This program should apply to those suppliers of a particular size — larger than appropriate for the card program, but too small for an SCF program (see Figure 4). While DPO extension is not possible with dynamic discounting, buying firms may extract additional discounts from suppliers and therefore positively affect cost of goods sold (COGS) on the income statement. Dynamic discounting may be used to lower purchase costs beyond the negotiated

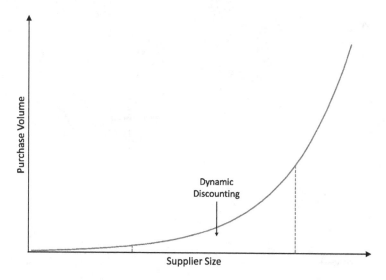

Figure 4: Targeting of Dynamic Discounting Programs

price. Therefore, it will be less effective with the smallest suppliers because the discount will contribute very little to improve overall COGS. Similarly, the largest suppliers will have power to resist the buyers' attempts to further extract discounts.

Lastly, supply chain finance programs are typically used for the largest suppliers who represent a large volume for the buying firm. Because the implementation takes a certain amount of onboarding, it is unlikely that a firm can use this for all of its suppliers. Most examples that we observed had a certain level of minimum sales for their suppliers to be eligible. Depending on the volume of the largest suppliers compared to the rest of the suppliers, some programs focused on roughly the top 50 suppliers. Nonetheless, we would like to point out that in some cases we saw many more suppliers that participated beyond these top suppliers. Figure 5, when compared to Figure 4, shows considerable overlaps involving mid-sized suppliers.

The overall strategy should be dependent on the goals of the firm. If DPO extension is the primary goal, then supply chain finance should be extended to as many suppliers as possible. It may be possible to push the boundaries to the extent that an adjacent card program becomes feasible.

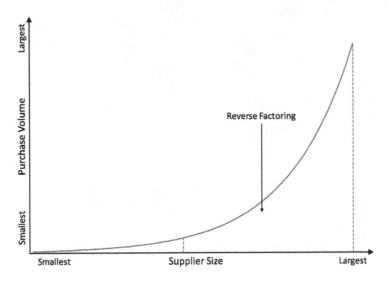

Figure 5:   Targeting of SCF Programs

That would eliminate the need for dynamic discounting. Conversely, if the firm's working capital is less of a limitation, then dynamic discounting can provide additional cost reductions. Depending on the need, it may be possible to bridge the card and supply chain finance programs with a dynamic discounting initiative.

The firm should select the appropriate tool to fit its financial strengths and the strength and structure of its supply chain. The tools presented above are current. It is likely that these tools will evolve as more options are added and new types of support fintechs are developed.

Payment Practices

Payments make up a significant part of the financial exchange between buyers and sellers, and payment practices should be viewed as an SCF issue rather than an accounting topic. According to the information we have collected, firms have inconsistent payment terms embedded in their contracts and orders. Some of them even have several different terms within a single supplier. While there may be business reasons to vary the contract terms, allowing a proliferation of terms across the supply base is usually unnecessary. This proliferation of terms makes it harder to manage the relationship, more difficult to process invoices, and adds a layer of often-unneeded complexity. One bank informed us that an unexpected value of its services is that it is able to help firms make their payment terms more consistent.

We examine payment practices from a number of perspectives as follows:

- length of payment terms,
- consistency of payment terms,
- invoice adjustments,
- invoice visibility,
- payment dispute resolution,
- offering of alternative funding options.

These categories were also used in an index constructed by Rutgers Business School.[1]

Length of Payment Terms

A number of firms have benchmarked their payment terms against their competitors. Currently, the averages vary widely by industry.[2] Some companies we talked to during our field research maintained the standard 2/10 net 30. Others had much higher ranges; for example, some automotive parts retailers paid their suppliers between 250 and 350 days after receipt of the goods. Further, in the consumer packaged goods industry, leading firms have moved already beyond 90 days toward 120-day payment terms. From the supplier's perspective, when they hear "terms extension," given the importance of cash flow, to many of them, to deliberately extend their

---

[1]Rudolf, L. and Sengun, Y. (2017). "The Rutgers Business School Payment Practices Index for the US Retail Industry." *Rutgers Business Review*, 2(1), 157–162.

[2]The Hackett Group (2018). "U.S. Cos. Improve Working Capital Performance." Retrieved from www.marketwatch.com/press-release/hackett-us-cos-improve-working-capital-performance-2018-07-19.

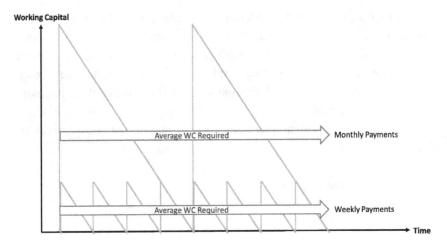

Figure 6:   Payment Timing

receivables seems unfair and often capricious. However, from the buying firm's perspective, when executives are asked to focus on the cash conversion cycle (CCC), they find themselves in a situation where ever-extending payment terms are necessary.

The timing of payments is another method of optimizing cash. One of the firms included in the research recently changed its payment timing to suppliers. Previously, this large buying firm accumulated supplier invoices over the course of a month and then paid those suppliers 60 days after the end of the accumulation period. They changed the payment timing to be weekly accumulations of supplier invoices plus 80 days. This change in payment policy resulted in reducing the cash on hand required. It is similar to changing the ordering of inventory from monthly orders to weekly orders. This logic can be seen graphically in Figure 6.

Consistency of Payment Terms

Some companies are very consistent in the manner in which they approve invoices and transmit their payments to suppliers, but this is more of an exception than the norm. Most often, payment terms within a buying firm across suppliers or even within the same supplier are typically inconsistent. However, this inconsistency can be a significant drawback for suppliers. Similar to inventory, they must hold excess cash to cover the uncertainty of how late a payment is received. One benefit of a supply chain financing program is to make payment terms more consistent.

Invoice Adjustments

Buyers may take invoice adjustments as a means of correcting deficits or issues with an order. For example, if an order has missing or defective items, those costs can be deducted from a payment. However, some suppliers perceive these adjustments, also called charges or chargebacks, as an unfair way to reduce costs after the delivery was made. In those cases, suppliers must spend time to appeal those adjustments. Often, these adjustments are made electronically, in a procure-to-pay system if certain criteria are not met.

Invoice Visibility

When suppliers submit invoices, it may be 90 days or more until the payment has been received. In that time, the supplier may not be aware of any issues with an invoice until they are contacted by the buyer or even until they receive a payment reflecting certain adjustments. Thus, it is important for buyers to not only provide their suppliers with updates, but to also have internal transparency about the status of invoices. Especially for companies who have made commitments to their suppliers it is important to have real-time visibility and control over those invoices. Technology can be helpful in providing visibility and several packages offer this functionality.

Payment Dispute Resolution

Similar to invoice visibility, in the event of a dispute it is important that a transparent process is in place in which suppliers can resolve any disputes the buyers have. Often, suppliers believe that companies routinely adjust payments of invoices to reflect certain charges and then place an undue burden on the supplier to prove its case, which is not only time consuming but also frustrating. In particular, smaller suppliers can have more difficulties following up on those issues. Especially, when it becomes routine, they can get the impression that these charges are leveled against them as a means of cost reduction, rather than being based on actual incidents with an order or invoice. Thus, companies that are committed to transparency in resolving disputes will be able to gain goodwill from their suppliers compared to their competitors who do not possess such transparency.

Offering of Alternative Funding Options

In the event that a supplier requires faster payment of invoices, does the buyer have options to offer payment quicker than usual? The techniques for this process have been described in previous chapters, but it is important to view this from a perspective of payment processes as well. Suppliers may face the need to obtain short-term funding and one source of that funding is accelerated invoice payment. Providing suppliers that flexibility will enable them to balance their funding needs with the ability of buyers to reduce cost. In fact, it can become a win–win for both sides if those processes are implemented and administered consistently.

Overall, buyers should carefully consider their payment practices, which will have an impact on the overall buyer–supplier relationship. It can enable firms to build goodwill, which will enable them to maintain better relationships. The suggestions outlined above do not require heavy investment, and most sophisticated organizations can easily implement them with existing technology.

Supplier Perspective of Supply Chain Financing

For the buying firm, there are several issues that should be considered from the supplier's perspective. First, there is often some resistance to moving away from the standard 2/10 net 30. This could simply stem from the fear of the unknown or expenses involved in implementing SCF programs. However, the supplier should be reminded that the early payment discount part of 2/10 net 30 can be quite expensive, because when viewed on an annualized basis, it is around 36 percent APR (200 BP × 365/20).

Moving to longer payment terms and offering SCF provides the supplier with early payments after invoice receipt at an annualized discount of around 2 percent. When compared to the cost of a commercial card transaction at around 250 BP for payment within two to three days, SCF is significantly cheaper.

Another, often forgotten, critical advantage of these SCF programs is that variability of payment is eliminated and structure around those payment flows are clear to all parties. It addresses one of the key challenges that buyers on the accounts payable side have — that they approve invoices and supplier terms on an *ad hoc* basis. Every invoice can be a new event. An invoice with 60-day net can be paid in 65 days or 80 days but rarely right on time. By moving to an SCF program, a consistent structure is imposed and the approval process is systematized. This is analogous to managing inventory. If sellers knew precisely when customers were buying a product, only that inventory would be necessary; however, since there is uncertainty, firms need to hold safety stock. Similarly, when supplier firms do not know when payments are going to be received, they need more working capital as a buffer to fund daily operations.

Chapter 7

Types of Firms Providing
SCF Services

There are primarily three types of companies involved in supply chain financing (SCF) — customer firms, supplier firms, and banks or other SCF providers. In Figure 1, the solid line from supplier firms to customer firms depicts the deliveries of goods and the broken line represents the flow of payment. This simple figure captures our view at the beginning of the research.

However, there is much more variety in the SCF provider category than many managers realize. For example, there are several types of networks that payment transactions can be routed through, such as ACH, credit cards, and wire transfers. In addition, payment flows can be complicated, especially if they are aided by the existence of fintech companies that have been very innovative in this area.

Banks

Banks have been involved in trade finance for centuries. Recently, SCF has emerged as an important low-risk source of loans for banks. Specific programs to facilitate buyer–supplier transactions have been developed to link the various parties in a transaction (i.e., the buyer, the seller, and a financing institution) to reduce costs and increase velocity of payment. SCF provides short-term credit that draws from the buying firm's access

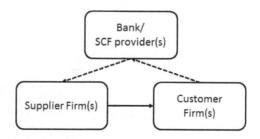

Figure 1:   Types of Firms in SCF

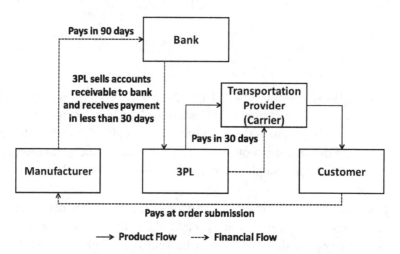

Figure 2:   SCF for Transportation Services

to credit. The supplier can use the buyer's cost of capital to take early payment while the buyer can extend payables. In this regard, the banks are
involved to facilitate the transaction and improve working capital for both
the buyer and the seller. For the banks, this is a low-risk loan to utilize the
balance sheet of a stable buying firm. In fact, it allows the bank to lend to
firms around the world that are not typically among its customer base. The
growing popularity of SCF is driven by the increasing globalization and
complexity of the supply chain.

Figure 2 shows an SCF transaction between an electronics firm (buyer)
and a 3PL (supplier) that is procuring transportation for the buying firm.

In this example, a large bank is providing early payment for the 3PL based on the buying firm's credit risk.

SCF encourages collaboration between the buyer and supplier, rather than making it harder to work together because of conflicting goals; that is to say, typically, the buyer attempts to extend payment as long as possible while the seller wants to be paid as soon as possible. SCF works best when the buyer has a better credit rating than the supplier and can access capital at a better credit risk level and, therefore, a lower cost. The buyer can leverage this superior position to negotiate an extension of payment terms, which enables the buyer to hold on to cash longer to use it for something else. The supplier benefits by accessing cheaper capital more quickly.

Table 1 lists several of the largest banks participating in SCF programs.

Table 1:   Largest Banks Active in SCF

Bank Name	Description of Program	Country
Bank of America	One of the largest banks in the United States. In addition to SCF, it also offers commercial credit card programs.	USA
Banco Santander	Offers a number of trade finance solutions to businesses.	Spain
BNP Paribas	Has specific expertise in commodities and receivables finance.	France
Citigroup	One of the first and largest SCF programs in the United States. It also offers commercial credit card programs, among others, such as freight processing.	USA
Deutsche Bank	Has specific expertise in receivables and distribution finance.	Germany
HSBC	One of the largest SCF programs globally.	UK
JPMorgan Chase	One of the largest banks in the United States. In addition to SCF, it also offers commercial credit card programs.	USA
Standard Chartered	Mostly specializes in working in developing economies, such as Africa, Asia, or the Middle East.	UK
Sumitomo Mitsui Banking Corporation	One of largest Asian banks active in trade finance with expertise in Europe, Africa, Middle East, Asia Pacific, and Latin America.	Japan

During the late 1990s, there was a push in the financial industry to develop new financial tools. SAP and Citigroup formed a joint venture (JV) to facilitate early payment for suppliers. The JV company was called Orbian and was what is now known as a "fintech" company. The plan was to connect the entire supply chain by effectively processing all transactions throughout the supply chain through this mechanism. Orbian and a similar firm, Prime Revenue, were gaining little attention from the market.[1] Citibank, as part of the Orbian JV, had the first working SCF program in place with Stanley Works. At the same time, firms like General Motors and General Electric had their own in-house reverse factoring programs. However, they relied on explicit guarantees by the buyer.

Commercial Credit Card Providers

An overview of offerings in the commercial credit card business is presented in Table 2. As previously mentioned, there are a number of parties involved in the processing of credit cards. Most corporate users have the choice of three networks: American Express, MasterCard, or Visa. With the latter two, firms enroll in a card program through an issuing bank, which are typically large financial firms, such as Bank of America, Citibank, JPMorgan Chase, or Wells Fargo in the United States. With American Express, the card is issued by the transmitter/processor. On the receiving end of the transaction is the merchant acquirer who has the relationship with the seller and receives the funds from the issuing bank. During the transaction the payment is routed from the issuer through an interchange network operated by American Express, MasterCard, or Visa, and then to the merchant acquirer, and finally to the seller. The buyer then pays its card issuer at the specified time.

Utilizing commercial cards is a fast method of purchasing. They allow the buying firm to reduce the time to procure with regular or new suppliers that are just being onboarded. They have become a tool that CPOs like because they also help capture revenue for the buying firm through rebates.

---

[1] Gustin, D. (2014). "A Disruptive Supply Chain Finance Vendor Fifteen Years Later — Who Is Orbian?" Retrieved from http://spendmatters.com/tfmatters/a-disruptive-supply-chain-finance-vendor-fifteen-years-later-who-is-orbian/.

Table 2: Sample Firms Involved in Card Transactions

Function	Examples
Issuer	American Express, Bank of America, Citigroup, JPMorgan Chase, Wells Fargo, etc.
Transmitter/Processor	American Express, MasterCard, Visa, etc.
Merchant Acquirer	First Data, Bank of America, Global Payments, JPMorgan Chase, etc.

Fintech Companies

Fintech firms are companies that utilize technology to reinvent financial systems and make funding the supply chain more efficient. They operate on technology platforms that use a funding source to connect with the buyer and supplier.

They are *not* banks. They are not under the same regulations as banks. Because of this, and their nature to be facilitated by technology advancement, they have been able to create innovative practices. These innovations have led to increased options for small- and medium-sized suppliers. Fintech firms have developed new procure-to-pay (P2P) capabilities. In some cases, they have become a buying firm's purchasing system and their services include cataloging of suppliers (a database of approved suppliers), PO transmission, and electronic invoicing and payment. In Figure 3, a sample P2P system is depicted. This diagram shows how early payment of invoices is enabled. Fintech firms have integrated with commercial credit card providers, or they can access a number of funders that can finance receivables at competitive interest rates. Some of these platforms have the ability to provide dynamic discounting.

The Dynamic Environment of Fintech Companies

The environment for fintech companies is rapidly evolving. Table 3, while not exhaustive, lists the significant players in this industry. In the future we anticipate a larger number of new entrants to become active in this space. Most companies on the list are less than 15 years old, with varying degrees of SCF capabilities. It is likely that in the future some fintechs

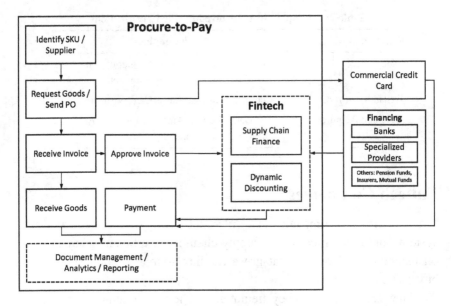

Figure 3:   Fintech Capabilities

will include procure-to-pay (P2P) functionality. As systems move quickly to SaaS and to the cloud, adding P2P functionality to a fintech platform, or adding supply chain finance capabilities to a purchasing system, will become commonplace.

It is also possible that a fintech that began or has expertise with a different system or management category will add SCF functionality. For example, SOVOS, which is a software/management system that specializes in tax management and compliance in Latin America, has recently begun building a supply chain finance platform to assist smaller suppliers to be able to manage slower payments from the buying firm as well as improving their complex tax compliance.

If we think about it for a moment, most of us have a fintech model on our phones. It is estimated that 63 percent of Americans have an app on their smart phone for a bank such as Citibank, Bank of America, Chase, etc.[2]

---

[2]Clabaugh, J. (2018). "Do You Have 'Fintech' on Your Phone? Most of Us Do." *WTOP*. Accessed February 19, 2018 at: https://wtop.com/business-finance/2018/02/fintech-on-your-phone/.

Table 3: Selected Fintech Companies

Firm	Specialization	Comments
Ant Financial	Former Alipay and is owned by the Chinese firm Alibaba	Ant Financial Services Group (former Alipay) is the payments arm of the Chinese Alibaba Group. It is the largest mobile and online payments platform in the world. Also includes Yu'e Bao, the largest money-market fund in the globe. Founded in 2015.
Basware	Procure-to-pay platform	A Finnish fintech software company selling enterprise software for financial processes, purchase-to-pay, and financial management.
C2FO	Exchange-based dynamic discounting/early payment	Similar concept to Priceline only for early payment of receivables. Target market is SME firms.
Fundera	Loan intermediary	Platform where businesses needing short-term working capital can apply to several potential lenders at the same time. Fundera is paid by the lender.
Funding Circle	Marketplace-based trade financing	Funding Circle is a marketplace that focuses on small businesses in the UK, USA, Germany, and the Netherlands. Firms can borrow directly from a wide range of investors, including more than 60,000 people, the UK government, local councils, universities, and a number of financial organizations.
GT Nexus/ Infor	Supply chain collaboration platform with some SCF functionality	Merged with TradeCard, another provider of SCF solutions. It was recently acquired by Infor, a provider of cloud-based software for businesses.

(Continued)

Table 3:   (*Continued*)

Firm	Specialization	Comments
Invoice Bazaar	Invoice Bazaar connects large suppliers with SME suppliers which allow them to get early payment on their receivables	Invoice Bazaar provides suppliers with working capital by digitizing the transactions which are done manually. Provides financing to a supplier by taking buyer risk. Provides supply chain finance, dynamic discounting, and receivables finance.
Klarna	Swedish fintech firm	Klarna takes on credit risk for retailers in exchange for a portion of the sale. Allows consumers to pay for online purchases after receiving the goods. Recently received a full banking license in Europe.
Lending Tree	Loan intermediary	Similar to Fundera, platform where businesses needing short-term working capital can apply to several potential lenders at the same time.
Maersk Trade Finance	Shipping line developing business to provide shippers working capital relief	Customers have access to trade finance if they are shipping via Maersk liners. Shipping containers are the collateral that Maersk uses to determine how much capital is to be provided.
Orbian	Supply chain financing	Early fintech company that started originally as a JV between SAP and Citibank. It finances the purchases of the receivables with financial partners under Clearstream, Euroclear, and DTC note issuances under no-purchase agreement.
PayPal Working Capital	PayPal-based supplier funding platform	PayPal Working Capital provides funding based on a supplier's PayPal sales history. No credit check on the supplier to receive funding so there is no effect on its credit score.

Table 3: (*Continued*)

Firm	Specialization	Comments
Paytm	Indian electronic payments company	Paytm is a mobile payments and commerce platform based in India. Began with online mobile recharge and bill payments and evolved to an online marketplace today. Has more than 230 million registered users.
PrimeRevenue	Supply chain financing and dynamic discounting	Technology platform that is widely considered to be the most robust. Its software can help analyze firm spend and provide a strategy to optimize payment terms based on multiple benchmarks and supplier characteristics. Technology includes payment terms optimization. In addition to SCF, can help firms do dynamic discounting.
SAP Ariba	Supply chain financing and dynamic discounting	Unit of SAP, that is providing a complete procure-to-pay capability.
SOVOS	Tax compliance platform company	Tax compliance firm that operates primarily in Latin America. Beginning to offer supply chain finance.
Taulia	Supply chain financing and dynamic discounting	A procure-to-pay platform that is independent of ERP software firms or banks. It is able to provide flexible options for buyers and sellers.
Textura	Supply chain financing	Concentrates on the construction industry. Value proposition for general contractor is higher quality process.
TRADE IX	Shared SCF platform that utilizes a blockchain distributed ledge	Solution has a platform infrastructure for banks, asset managers, B2B networks, and value-added service providers. Built on distributed ledger technology, the platform utilizes blockchain.

Those apps were developed by fintech companies and adopted by large banks. While it does not seem that those specific apps are relevant to supply chain finance, they are used millions of times every day to help manage both personal and business transfers that facilitate the purchase of goods and services.

Blockchain

While banks and other financial institutions are excited about blockchain and its promise of making many of their systems more productive and efficient, there is also nervousness that banks can eventually be disintermediated because of the power of this technology. Some banks will have great difficulty changing their business processes and will try to have the distributed ledger platform adapt to their current processes. This will likely leave them open to disintermediation from startup firms that will develop new processes without the current overhead that these banks and financial institutions will have a hard time disposing of.

Banks and Disintermediation

Blockchain was initially treated with skepticism by banks and other financial institutions.[3] After realizing that distributed ledger technology had the potential of disintermediating banks and other financial institutions, they began to think about how they could utilize the technology to make certain kinds of transactions much more efficient. For example, blockchain platforms could greatly reduce the cost and increase the speed of trade finance transactions such as bills of lading or letters of credit.

Blockchains can be very useful in these types of transactions because numerous parties need access to the exact same information. Plus, the traditional paper-based letters of credit or bills of lading can easily be lost or mishandled. Currently, many of these trade finance transactions are still executed with fax machines, where the parties need a physical stamp

---

[3] Martin, A. (2017). "Five Ways Banks Are Using Blockchain." *Financial Times*, October 16, 2017. Retrieved from https://www.ft.com/content/615b3bd8-97a9-11e7-a652-cde3f882dd7b.

on a piece of paper. This is a very important part of supply chain management. If a firm is shipping product from Asia, it could be that the paperwork may need to be accessed by as many as 50 people.[4] This would include not only the shippers and the shipping companies but also the agents, customs house brokers, freight providers, ports insurers, and customs officials. Implementing a blockchain platform that would digitize logistics transactions and flows could greatly improve the productivity of entities facilitating transactions. Some of the firms that are working to digitize the bill of lading process are Shipchain, Wave, EssDocs, and Bolero.[5]

When a firm raises money via a loan, it can be a long time before the transaction is eventually executed. On average, short-term loans associated with trade finance can take up to three or four weeks. Much of the communication around these loans is still executed via fax machine and messenger documents. Several banks are forming consortiums to start putting loans such as these on distributed ledger platforms. As most CPOs know, trade finance and the financial flows behind supply management are generally inefficient.

Financial settlements in supply chains can take longer than mortgage processing. This is largely driven by payment policies to optimize cash flows, but there are improvements to be made in the automation and settlement of payments along with supply chain financing and letters of credit. A blockchain-based system could provide the ability to confirm availability, receipt of goods, payments, etc., in real time and reduce the manual intervention, reducing these transactions to seconds instead of months. This can take latency, cost, and lack of trust out of the system.

The opportunity to improve financial liquidity across supply networks via blockchain technologies is potentially a game-changer for supply networks. Several new blockchain applications are incorporating supply chain finance capabilities. Sweetbridge,[6] a startup firm in Scottsdale, Arizona, is working on providing liquidity to suppliers in a

---

[4] *Ibid.*

[5] *Ibid.*

[6] https://sweetbridge.com.

supply chain financing arrangement utilizing distributed ledger systems. Their goal is to improve settlement times, increase liquidity in supply networks, and remove cost with smart payments. When suppliers receive an order, their weighted cost of capital is somewhere in the 6–10 percent range (for most suppliers). They finance the cost of acquiring components to produce the product ordered until the customer receives and pays for the product, which can be a long period of time as most buying firms are extending their payables cycles. This cost of capital expense is passed to the next tier of suppliers and so on, in descending fashion, with each supplier bearing the expense for several weeks or months. A great deal of working capital is tied up in supply chains. The bulk of working capital is inventory, payables, and receivables, and reducing unnecessary working capital has become the job of supply managers.

There is the potential to eliminate much of the need of this working capital and improve margins simply by replacing this traditional funding mechanism with blockchain-enabled token-based financing for supply networks. These tokens would come with embedded intelligence, unlike traditional currency. Smart tokens can include security measures along with instructions about payment terms, conditions, and processes to initialize upon payment. With tokens, payments are recognized immediately across multiple supply chain tiers and fees are greatly reduced.

Limiting Factors of Blockchains

Blockchain appears to be a technology that will have a large impact on the supply chain at some point in the future. The adoption of blockchain within procurement organizations is likely to be slow. Scaling and transaction throughput is an important challenge that needs to be solved for blockchain networks to operate efficiently and sustain growing adoption. For public blockchain platforms, the cost of consensus needs to be lowered in order for wide adoption. The mass of transactions in a large enterprise both slows down the network and reveals a lot of information to the public. There are many barriers that will have to be worked through before blockchains become a technology that people are using for mission-critical applications. The early applications of blockchain tend to be specialized.

Non-Traditional Funders of SCF Programs

From an investment perspective, receivables financing is an attractive short-term investment. Naturally, numerous types of investors are attracted to it. Insurance companies, retirement systems, and mutual funds are very interested in buying this type of high-quality debt. They are able to gain higher rates of return than traditional treasury bills, for example, and they provide a short investment timeframe. Most of these investors use funders, such as the ones shown in Table 4, to access the investment opportunities in SCF. A list of funders is shown in Table 4. These companies are looking at SCF programs for short-term, low-risk returns. They are expanding quickly beyond the traditional full-service banks.

Table 4:   Selected Non-Bank Supply Chain Funders

Name	Specialty	Countries
Advance Global Capital	Funding SMEs in the emerging markets throughout the world.	UK
Apex Peak	Funding for SMEs throughout Singapore and in South Africa.	Singapore
Greensill Capital	Principal investor group specializing in structured trade finance, working capital optimization, specialty financing, and contract monetization.	Australia, UK, and United States
GemCorp	Investment fund focused on emerging markets in Africa, Asia, and Europe across sectors and asset classes.	UK
Propel	Provides working capital solutions, such as supplier finance and receivables finance to firms in African countries.	South Africa
Tower Trade Group	Supply chain finance and IT services for companies in Ireland, South Africa, Spain, Switzerland, UK, and the United States.	Switzerland

Funding Mechanisms

There are several methods by which these programs can be funded. Banks can operate their own SCF programs or act as funders for a fintech firm. They can also syndicate loans, where several banks can partner and pool their capital in an SCF program. This can be transparent to the buyer or it may occur outside of the buying firm's influence.

Banks perform other duties as well. For example, Orbian, a fintech, converts the approved invoices to Depository Trust Corporation (DTC) notes, which are essentially derivatives of the cash flow between buyer and seller. These notes are then sold to banks who are looking for low-risk, high-velocity instruments in which to invest. Similarly, they use Clearstream or Euroclear, often in conjunction with international companies. Other fintech companies, such as PrimeRevenue, use special purpose vehicles (SPVs) to enable the multi-bank funding. These fintech companies are able to use non-bank funders such as pension funds and insurance companies. They often collaborate with banks such as Citigroup and HSBC that have agency and trust departments as part of their offerings, and through those mechanisms they are able to ensure compliance to the terms of the financing arrangement. More on compliance is discussed in Chapter 8.

Chapter 8

Macro Issues Affecting Supply Chain Financing

Regulation

The compliance environment is tough. Banks are finding compliance to be difficult because they not only have an oversight on things such as mortgages but they also have to act as police for money laundering. They must act as enforcers of the anti-money laundering (AML) rules and ensure that corporations and individuals do not use the banking systems as a vehicle to launder money or for other fraudulent activities. In the first quarter of 2015, legal expenses for one large global bank were $2.7 billion. In addition to these legal expenses, it had to incur a substantial expense to monitor compliance and ensure it was adhering to regulations around the world. Banking has become a very complex business across the industry. In the last 15 years, regulation around banks has dramatically increased both in the United States and globally. Banks are very concerned about appropriate behavior with respect to not facilitating drug trafficking, preventing money laundering, and ensuring their customers are doing the right thing. Banks are one of the few tools that allow a government to see if members of the supply chain might be breaking the law.

We anticipate that the amount of global regulation around the supply chain will continue to grow. Legislation such as Dodd–Frank and Sarbanes–Oxley have changed how companies can operate their supply chains both in the United States and around the world. Almost all multinational companies have had to strengthen their compliance functions to deal with all of the increased regulations being written by governments. Purchasing managers need to take an active role in understanding how regulations impact both the supply chain and financial management.

There are several regulatory pieces that must be satisfied before a bank can implement supply chain financing (SCF) programs. One of the pieces of regulation is "know your customer" (KYC). KYC is the regulation in the United States whereby a bank must verify the identity of its clients. It is applied to all banks and many financial firms. The purpose of this regulation is to ensure that customers provide detailed anti-corruption due diligence and to prevent identity theft, financial fraud, money laundering, and terrorist financing. These regulations have become increasingly important to help businesses avoid problems with identity theft, money laundering, and, most seriously, financing terrorism. Banks and financial entities in the United States are spending hundreds of millions of dollars to manage and update information that has to be redone with every new regulation. Demand for professionals to manage KYC compliance is rising, but there are not enough individuals with the proper compliance training to support all the banks' requirements.

Another important regulation is AML. Money laundering is the process of making "dirty" money appear legal. Money laundering facilitates crimes such as drug trafficking and terrorism. Banks have to show that programs they develop are compliant with AML. Regulations have been strengthened over the years to develop more tools to combat money laundering.

Table 1 shows the most relevant types of regulations to SCF. Among them, the AML laws require banks to collect some of the following information on their customers: the nature of business; the purpose of relationship with bank; expected pattern of activity; the business' supply chain trading partners upstream and downstream; and information about the business' reputation or references. This requirement becomes relevant during the onboarding process of SCF, because it is costly for the banks to perform this regulatory compliance.

Table 1:   Key Regulations Affecting SCF

Regulation	Impact
AML	Guidelines to protect and prevent commercial banks from being used by criminal elements for illegal and money laundering activities, intentionally or unintentionally. The regulation has recently also included measures to prevent identity theft, financial fraud, and terrorist financing.
Basel III[a]	Reforms to strengthen global capital and liquidity rules with the goal of promoting a more resilient banking sector. The objective of the reforms is to improve the banking sector's ability to absorb shocks arising from financial and economic stress, whatever the source, thus reducing the risk of spillover from the financial sector to the real economy. The Basel III regulations are capital requirements on banks.
Customer Identification Program (CIP)	The first step in any KYC program is a bank's CIP which requires a bank to collect and document a customer's name, date of birth, address, and identification presented.
Customer Due Diligence (CDD)	The second step is CDD which requires the bank to obtain information to verify the customer's identity and assess the risk. If the CDD inquiry leads to a high-risk determination, the bank has to conduct an Enhanced Due Diligence (EDD).
Dodd Frank	Recent regulation approved as a response to the Great Recession, this brought significant changes to financial regulation in the United States. It changes the existing regulatory structure in an effort to streamline and enhance the regulatory process, increasing oversight of specific institutions regarded as a systemic risk or "too big to fail."
KYC	A bank has to verify the identity of its clients. The purpose of this regulation is to ensure that customers provide detailed anti-corruption due diligence and prevention of identity theft, financial fraud, money laundering, and terrorist financing.
Uniform Commercial Code (UCC) Checks	In the United States, the UCC governs private transactions including receivables — in different countries different regulations apply. By allowing lenders to take a security interest on a collateral owned by a debtor's asset, the law provides lenders with a legal relief in case of default by the borrower. With such legal remedy available, lenders would therefore be able to lend capital at lower interest rates. In all 50 states, Article 9 of the UCC governs secured transactions where security interests are taken.

[a]Basel Committee on Banking Supervision (2011). Basel III: A global regulatory framework for more resilient banks and banking systems, p. 1.

There has been much discussion recently about deregulating the banks again. During the beginning of the Trump administration in the United States, the new administration looked for several means by which to reduce regulation of all kinds. It remains to be seen if the efforts to deregulate are successful in the long run.

Accounting Treatment of SCF

The accounting treatment of SCF programs, in general, has been a hotly debated issue. Robert Comerford, who at the time was a professional accounting fellow in the SEC's Office of the Chief Accountant (OCA), addressed the issue in a series of speeches in 2003 and 2004.[1] The speeches outlined some general guidelines around how SCF programs should be treated from an accounting standpoint. The key issue is whether these programs are resulting in additional accounts payables for the buyer or if they have to be classified as a loan from the buyer to the supplier. There are certain conditions when they have to be accounted for as a loan. First, if the buyer makes guarantees to the bank that it doesn't make to its suppliers. Second, if the bank or financial institution is paying buyers so-called "marketing payments" that compensate them for advertising the program to their suppliers. Another way to look at this issue is the sharing of rebates between the buyer and the financial institution. However, some viewed Comerford's remarks as being directed toward banks and not being relevant for fintechs.[2] As a result, several buying firms stopped their pursuit of SCF because they were not certain how to classify these arrangements. Often, the case of Alcoa in 2003 is cited as a reason why these programs might not have been effective.[3]

---

[1] Comerford, R. J. (2004). "Speech by SEC Staff: Remarks before the 2004 AICPA National Conference on Current SEC and PCAOB Developments." Retrieved from www.sec.gov/news/speech/spch120604rjc.htm.

[2] Kramer, R. (2017). "Supply Chain Finance Accounting Myths and Reality." *The Secured Lender*. Retrieved from www.thesecuredlender-digital.com/thesecuredlender/march_2017?pg=22#pg22.

[3] Hintze, J. (2012). "Supplier Finance Accounting Issues: Some Third-party Arrangements Could Mean Reclassifying Payables as Loans." *Treasury & Risk*, www.treasuryandrisk.com/2012/05/02/supplier-finance-accounting-issues.

In other countries, however, accounting rules might be different, allowing companies to deviate from SEC rules. For example, in the UK, phone operator Vodafone invested more than $1 billion dollars into a fund, jointly run by the Swiss asset manager GAM Holding AG and London-based Greensill Capital.[4] The fund then offered Vodafone's suppliers an early payment option on an invoice in return for a discount. As an investor in the fund, Vodafone is able to make a return on its capital. In addition, in the recent years, its DPO have grown from the mid-20s in 2003 to almost 50 in 2018. It seems that as of 2019, there are no accounting issues with this program.

It is possible to proceed with SCF without running into accounting issues. To assess the true value of the program, the financials need to be entered appropriately as loans or accounts payable on the buyer's balance sheet. The following steps help ensure proper procedures. First, it is important to dissociate the initiative of extending payment terms from the early payment financing. Second, it is important to avoid tri-party agreements, such as agreements between the buyer, seller, and funder simultaneously. Rather, programs should be kept as independent arms-length agreements. Third, buyers should always pay the invoice on the maturity date as stated and resist early payments with discounts shared with the bank and no prolonged payment terms with interest payments to the bank. Fourth, the buying firm should resist asking for any kind of returns or rebates from the bank or fintech company that is managing its program. Fifth, the buying firm should be hands-off regarding which funder is buying particular invoices, or better yet have no direct knowledge of the funders. Overall, firms must be cautious how the program is managed, but in terms of the accounting treatment it can be managed equally well by a bank or by an independent multi-bank fintech platform. See Table 2 for a summary of the previous steps.

---

[4] Beardsworth, T. (2019). "Vodafone Invests in Fund Making Money Off Its Own Late Payments." *Bloomberg*, www.bloomberg.com/news/articles/2019-03-18/vodafone-finds-a-novel-investment-to-make-money-off-its-suppliers.

Table 2:   Key Steps to Ensure Correct Accounting Treatment of SCF Programs

1. Dissociate the initiative of extending payment terms from the early payment financing.

2. Avoid tri-party agreements; rather, keep as independent arms-length agreements.

3. Always pay the invoice on the maturity date as stated and resist early payments with discounts shared with the bank, and have no prolonged payment terms with interest payments to the bank.

4. The buying firm should resist asking for returns or rebates from the bank or fintech company that is managing its program.

5. The buying firm should be hands-off regarding which funder is buying particular invoices.

Interest Rates

For reverse factoring that is buyer-backed, the APR interest rate is based on the buyer's credit profile. For investment-grade companies, APR interest rates would likely be in the neighborhood of 8 percent or less. Nearly all of the SCF programs in the market today entail short-term financing of generally fewer than 180 days, but more typically 60 days. Currently, for five-year investment-grade loans and bonds, the price point is around 5–8 percent for multi-year borrowings, so logically, short-term funding would be less. For example, current interest rates for these arrangements are derived by cost of funds plus spread. The cost of funds is typically indexed to the LIBOR. The spread is a risk premium, based on the credit-worthiness of the buyer. If the 30-day short-term LIBOR is around 0.18 percent (APR) and credit spreads are around 1 percent, then the all-in rate for financing is an annualized 1.18 percent, or effectively 0.19 percent for 60 days.

In 2015, base rates worldwide were at or near zero. In the United States, in early 2019 the prime rate was currently around 3 percent, and borrowings often are some factor above or below this benchmark. Still, using "prime plus a premium" is, in 2019, below 8 percent in most cases. In fact, in Switzerland and the rest of Europe, central banks are offering negative yields on deposits or bonds. In other words, people are paying for the right to hold a government bond instead of the government paying the holder of the bond any interest.

If a supplier who is not in the Fortune 500 wants to obtain financing on its own, interest rates might be in the 8 percent all-in range depending on the credit profile and cash flows of the supplier. Commercial cards or p-cards offer a 2 percent fee reduction to get paid early. For example, if terms are around 30 days, this equates to an APR of about 24 percent ($365/30 \times 2$ percent), but the amounts are small and the supplier is not borrowing but accepting a discount to close its receivable. Also, factoring companies would be charging against the supplier's credit (assuming it is non-investment grade) with receivables used as collateral. These rates could be as high as 15 percent APR, if not more. Overall, since the buying companies are investment grade and they can borrow in today's market at historically low rates, these SCF programs are especially attractive to small- and medium-sized enterprises (SMEs).

Chapter 9

Supply Chain Management Meets Financial Statements

Supply chain professionals are often removed from financial outcomes due to organizational structures that are highly departmentalized and compartmentalized. This phenomenon can remove direct linkages, but the connection between supply chain and company profitability needs to be understood. In general, supply chain management has direct accountability over sourcing, manufacturing, and logistics. This means that most activities that have influence over the products and services reside within the domain of supply chain management. These activities have a strong influence over product quality, service quality, and operational efficiency. Inventory management is under the control of supply chain executives, which must balance inventory service levels and costs.

We have come full circle. At the beginning of this book, we offered an overview of basic financial concepts. This chapter will expand on those basic concepts and describe how the key financial statements such as the income statement (or profit and loss statement) and balance sheet are impacted by supply chain activities and affect movement of money and SCF-related activities.

Income Statement

The income statement provides the public with information about a firm's ability to achieve a profit. In addition to the income statement, companies also issue a balance sheet, which provides the public with an indication of how the company generates a profit by showing what properties it owns and obligations it owes. The cash flow statement is the third main financial statement and it highlights the firm's cash position by showing all sources of cash as well as uses of cash. An overview of how supply chain activities affect the company's financials is presented in Table 1.

Revenue

The top line of the income statement is sales (or revenue) and there are several ways in which supply chain activities can affect it. They are summarized below and in Table 2.

An effective supply chain will facilitate on-time delivery of complete orders, retain and strengthen customer relationships, and increase customer satisfaction, loyalty, and repeat purchases. To help increase revenue, supply chain can facilitate easily available products and services that are superior to competitors' products. When the supply chain results in strong relationships with the customer, revenues will grow. This not only satisfies customers' needs, but it can make it more difficult for customers to switch to a competitor. Overall, this will improve the desirability of the supplier to its customers and have an overall positive effect on market share. Supply chain processes, including increasing switching costs, makes a buyer more likely to continue to purchase from its current supplier.

A supplier who enables financing for a buyer to sell its products will find that it will drive sales as well. Similar to car manufacturers offering their customers financing options to go along with the car they purchase, suppliers who may have a financing advantage can leverage that advantage to incent customers to purchase from them and not their competitors. Firms that manage their supply chains well are able to provide their customers with "fresher" product offerings. They will be able to move products faster to market, which is more attractive to customers.

Firms can improve the selection of products and services (mix) that is offered to customers in a manner that maximizes revenue for the firm. One method where the supply chain can help is through SKU rationalization, where the firm reviews the performance of the different product offerings and reduces its number of SKUs. This removes unprofitable products

Table 1:   How Supply Chain Activities Affect Financials

Financial Categories	Supply Chain Management Activities
Income Statement	
Sales/Revenue	• Procure, create, and deliver value that customers are willing to pay for • Manage and deliver product and service mix offered to customers • Decrease lost sales through improved product availability • Decrease markdowns and reduce returns through improved inventory management
Cost of Goods Sold	• Sourcing • Manufacturing
Overhead (Sales, General & Administrative) Costs	• Marketing • Logistics • HR • IT • Finance and accounting • Research and development
Balance Sheet	
Assets	• Current assets • Non-current (fixed) assets
Accounts Receivable	• Reduce accounts receivable through faster payment
Cash and Cash Equivalents	• Funding the organization — supply chain is a critical element in generating cash for the firm • Utilizing the supply chain capabilities and structure more strategically generates more cash
Inventory	• Improve forecasting and demand planning • Reduce safety stock • Reduce raw material, WIP, and finished goods inventory • Reduce obsolete inventory • Reduce non-cost-of-money components of inventory carrying costs
Plant, Property, and Equipment	• Improve asset utilization and rationalization • Optimize equipment utilization • Improve plants and warehouses utilization and rationalization • Capacity planning • Lease/buy
Other Assets	• Improve investment planning and deployment
Liabilities	• Accounts payable • Financial liabilities
Accounts Payables (AP)	• Lengthen payment terms to hold on to cash longer • Better procurement strategies can positively impact AP

Table 2:   Impact of SCM on Sales/Revenues

- Create value that customers are willing to buy
  - Supply chain processes increase switching costs
  - Offer "fresher" product
- Improve product and service mix offered to customers
  - SKU rationalization
  - Rationalize services provided to customers
- Avoid lost sales
  - Improve product availability
  - Improve order fill rates
  - Reduce stockouts
  - Maximize purchases with financing options
- Increasing markdowns and reducing returns
  - Improve "drains" and move inventory
  - Recover value

from its sales offerings, as well as shifts the overall purchases to more profitable products. The firm might also rationalize services provided to customers. This means that the firm will actively evaluate what services customers receive and whether these services have an overall positive effect on revenue and profitability.

A key strategy to increase revenue is avoiding lost sales. Lost sales can be diminished through improvements in product availability. Retailers with superior in-stock availability appeal more to customers, especially at a time when most stores will allow consumers to check availability even before stepping into the building. In-stock availability is a critical strategy for many retailers. Walmart has prioritized their product availability and views it as important as low costs.[1]

Another related challenge is improving order fill rates. Fill rates are defined as the percentage of items on an invoice that are shipped from inventory (in other words not backordered). Companies that manage to maintain superior fill rates are able to maintain higher customer satisfaction levels. A related issue to improved fill rates are stockouts, which are

---

[1] www.forbes.com/sites/paularosenblum/2014/04/15/walmarts-out-of-stock-problem-only-half-the-story/#21a0ae867369.

defined as a temporary unavailability of inventory for a given SKU. Persistent and frequent stockouts lead to lost sales. If companies can offer their suppliers financing options, this should lead to suppliers being better able to fulfill orders for their customers. This is similar to car manufacturers and dealerships offering financing as an add-on service to their customers, which makes it significantly easier for customers to afford new cars.

Revenue is impacted by increasing inventory velocity and reducing product returns. A critical part of inventory management is to ensure adequate velocity of SKUs. In other words, firms must be able to flow inventory quickly through the supply chain to their customers. Due to rapid technological change, most products lose their value over time. The quicker a firm moves product out of its inventory to its customer the stronger its revenue will be. In addition, because most firms have limited warehousing space, the need to move inventory to make space for new items is important so that flow will not become obstructed.

For example, Nike has a very structured system of managing its inventory. When a new sneaker is introduced in its Niketown flagship stores and through its most important retailer partners, sales are closely monitored. If they do not meet a prescribed level, that SKU will get moved to other outlets, such as factory outlet stores, where it will first be discounted at around 30 percent and will receive further discounts over time if it does not sell. This strategy ensures that the inventory in the flagship stores and key retail partners is always fresh to keep interest levels high.

Returns management can significantly impact revenue generation. For decades, US retailers have recognized that the ability to easily return items can significantly impact the willingness of customers to purchase an item. As such, liberal return policies have become commonplace in US retail and represent an average of 6 percent of all sold products. However, if a company can reduce this percentage it represents a significant impact on revenue. The impact is often greater for the manufacturer who simply gets charged for the return by the retailer. A great deal of product returns in consumer electronics are due to customers' difficulty in setting up the product. Manufacturers have revised their products and implemented quick-start guides to combat that frustration. Overall, returns management can have a significant impact on revenue, but companies often don't manage it at all. When returns do occur, there are several strategies companies can use to recover value.[2]

Cost of Goods Sold

Cost reductions have traditionally been viewed as the main contribution of supply chain management. Most supply chain organizations tend to focus on cost, given a particular customer service level of performance. In other words, executives "set" a service level and supply chain professionals have to meet that service level at the lowest possible cost. The following section will be a review of the different areas where cost reductions are most likely to be found. As captured in Table 3, the focus will be on the categories of sourcing and manufacturing.

Sourcing, which has almost complete control over direct materials used to manufacture a firm's products, has the greatest potential to impact cost reduction. In general, cost reduction is one of the main performance metrics used to evaluate a purchasing department. Of course, cost reductions without concern to other factors, such as quality and service level, can be detrimental to the firm overall. Regardless, due to the relative magnitude of direct materials in many companies, any reduction in the cost base will have a significant impact on cost of goods sold. However, in most companies that have placed an emphasis solely on cost reductions, there will be a time when further cost reductions will no longer be possible at the same rate. In addition, the purchasing department is usually responsible for indirect materials, services, and capital goods. Through effective purchasing techniques, additional savings can be realized in those areas as well. In addition to the costs of direct and indirect materials, it is possible that a company manages and executes the movement and storage of those materials into the company's manufacturing facilities. Those costs would be considered costs of goods sold, while the outbound movement is covered under sales, general, and administrative costs, as discussed later on in this chapter. A related strategy is to focus on asset reductions, rather than cost reductions, in which companies shed assets

---

[2]Rogers, D. S. and Ronald S. T.-L. (1999). *Going Backwards: Reverse Logistics Trends and Practices*, Vol. 2, Reverse Logistics Executive Council, Pittsburgh, PA.

Table 3:   Impact of SCM on Cost of Goods Sold

Sourcing
- Reduce cost of direct materials
- Reduce cost of indirect materials, services, and capital goods
- Utilize supply chain to develop "virtual vertical integration"

Manufacturing
- Improve manufacturing processes
- Improve plant productivity
  - Improve scheduling
  - Reduce setup and changeover costs
  - Reduce number of last-minute production changes

- Improve production quality
  - Eliminate claims and reduce customer complaints
  - Reduce waste and rework
  - Improve management of warranty, replacement, and repair programs

and outsource. This will increase cost of goods sold, but when viewed under the auspices of economic value added, this strategy can be successful, even while increasing variable costs.

Some companies, such as Apple, Inc., have used their sourcing relationships to create supply networks based on virtual vertical integration. They will sometimes loan and sometimes lease manufacturing equipment into their suppliers' facilities to be used for the purpose of manufacturing their products.[3] For Apple, this ensures that it receives the most competitive price on raw materials and supplies. In addition, these arrangements provide a further benefit to Apple. Suppliers would be able to gain additional production capacity, while Apple is able to protect its supply chain from competitors building relationships with its suppliers. This is an adaptation of increasing volume for discounts. These strong supply chain relationships were able to protect Apple in the past from competitors such as HP/Palm gaining access to the most up-to-date components.[4] Because Apple had purchased most of the capacity, suppliers would not be able to

---

[3] http://www.theinvestor.co.kr/view.php?ud=20170714000483.
[4] https://www.theverge.com/2012/6/5/3062611/palm-webos-hp-inside-story-pre-postmortem.

supply other companies who competed with Apple without significant investment from the customer.

In manufacturing, a company can achieve significant efficiencies through streamlining its manufacturing operations. This can occur in several different ways, but regardless of the path chosen, the strategy must be consistently executed. For example, one company could be following a lean strategy, while another may choose to focus on economies of scale. Both strategies can be successful if they are executed properly and applied to the right economic environment. Regardless of the strategy, the overall goal is to improve plant productivity. This can occur in a number of ways. Scheduling could be one of the ways in which overall productivity can be enhanced. By ensuring that each step in the manufacturing process is sequenced with minimal wait time after the preceding step, the throughput of a given plant can be optimized. In addition, if batch sizes of manufactured products are optimized, then the plant would be able to minimize setup and changeover costs. In a lean environment, the whole manufacturing system would be set up to rarely require changeovers at all. Finally, if supply and demand are matched, then there is little need for last minute production changes which negatively impact the efficiency of the overall production system.

One of the main goals of manufacturing is to produce products with flawless quality. Early in the development of manufacturing, companies thought that quality was a detraction from overall efficiency; in other words, it was thought to be costly. Not until the rapid advancement of Japanese manufacturers, especially in the automotive industry, did that mind-set change. It was quite a groundbreaking thought when Phil Crosby said, as published in his book *Quality is Free* in 1979, that striving for perfection in manufacturing could be positive for overall manufacturing cost. In conjunction with the efforts by other quality experts, such as W. Edwards Deming and Joseph Juran, there was a collective shift in best practices. The idea was that if quality was part of every aspect of the manufacturing process, then not only would it be an overall improvement in manufacturing costs but also an improvement in overall customer satisfaction, which can save cost on addressing issues that arose due to poor quality. Specifically, claims and customer complaints will be reduced. Waste in the production process through overprocessing and rework will be reduced. By not producing an item correctly the first time, additional time, materials, labor, and machinery will be used to correct the problem. Finally, the costs of warranty, potential replacement of defective items, as well as repair programs will be reduced if quality is improved.

Overhead or Sales, General, and Administrative Costs

Overhead or sales, general, and administrative (SG&A) costs are reported on the income statement as the sum of all direct and indirect expenses of selling the products and services of the company, as well as all general and administrative expenses required to manage the company. Supply chain management can have a positive impact on overhead costs. There are several categories that comprise this section of the income statement, such as marketing and sales, logistics, human resources, information technology, finance/accounting, and research and development. These areas are detailed below and summarized in Table 4.

- **Marketing and sales:** Marketing and sales expenses usually make up a large portion of the total SG&A category. The major impact that supply chain management has on this category is that superior execution of the supply chain can reduce the need for aggressive selling and marketing efforts. Customers may choose a company based on its superior delivery service quality.[5] In general, this effect is poorly understood, as it is difficult for most companies to see the effects of logistics and supply chain activities on the overall marketing effort. It is the task of supply chain management professionals to show the value of their efforts.
- **Logistics:** In logistics, there are several areas where cost savings can be spread across the entire logistics network, from manufacturing plants to customers, consisting of distribution centers and transportation lanes. If the company manages any of the inbound logistics, those costs would be considered as costs of goods sold, but the general logic applies to both inbound and outbound logistics. In many companies, this is a vast network of facilities, machinery, equipment, and of course

---

[5]Leuschner, R. and Lambert, D. M. (2016). "Establishing Logistics Service Strategies that Increase Sales," *Journal of Business Logistics*, 37, 247–270.

Table 4:   Impact of SCM on Overhead/Sales, General, and Administrative Costs

Marketing
- Reduce need for aggressive selling and marketing efforts

Logistics
- Optimize physical network/facilities
- Leverage new and/or alternative distribution channels
- Streamline order processing and information flow with customer
- Reduce customer service costs by ensuring tasks are completed correctly the first time
- Prevent stockouts and expedited shipments
- Reduce order cycle time
- Leverage transportation and consolidate shipments
- Reduce loading and packaging requirements
- Reduce handling costs

Human Resources
- Reduce SCM staffing needs
- Reduce training needs
- Reduce benefit management needs

IT
- Reduce information systems costs

Finance and Accounting
- Reduce the need for administrative work due to supply chain errors
- Reduce the need for resources to obtain capital

Research and Development
- Reduce market introduction costs
- Reduce supplier search costs

a great number of people. Simply having this network in place requires a significant investment in terms of direct costs, however, through efficient and effective management of the function, there are significant cost savings possible.

One possibility would be to optimize the logistics network in terms of facilities and locations. When undertaking such optimizations, two major questions need to be addressed: (1) how many facilities are needed, and (2) where are those facilities located. In general, more facilities are costlier but improve customer service levels. The overall goal of logistics network optimization is to balance the two conflicting objectives. The other reason a company may want to optimize its logistics network would be to take advantage of new alternative distribution channels. In times when most retailers are trying to figure out what "omni-channel" means to their businesses, connecting the different distribution channels is one of the main challenges. Those new distribution channels often are costly to set up and operate, and thus must be carefully managed to ensure they can achieve cost reduction goals over time.

A large part of the order processing and fulfillment process is managed by the logistics function in most companies. Each time an order is placed, there are a number of steps that must be completed in order to move an order from receipt to fulfillment. With so many moving parts, there is great opportunity for improvement, as well as increasing the opportunities for cost reductions in the future as technology streamlines the process. Another important aspect of this process is to ensure quality of execution. This means that customers receive their orders on time and in full every time. Such a goal has the potential to reduce customer service costs by reducing the resources spent on fixing problems after they occur. In addition, this would also prevent the company from stocking out or having to expedite orders to meet promises made to customers.

It is fairly simple to measure the time from order receipt through successful delivery, also known as order cycle time. By reducing cycle time, not only is the current logistics system able to increase the orders throughput, but it can also improve lead times, which is valuable to customers.

Finally, logistics also has a physical component involving warehousing and transportation, in which cost savings can occur. Firms can leverage their transportation spend to gain better pricing from their carriers. There are several ways in which this can be done. One would be to pool transportation and send fewer, larger shipments. Particularly if those shipments can be combined into full truckloads, the savings can be significant. However, it not always necessary to change shipments to realize savings; simply providing a carrier with more volume might warrant savings across the whole network. There is an old saying in logistics that the two things firms should never ship are air and water. While customers nowadays are willing to spend considerable amounts for specialty water, it may not hold; however, "shipping air" can still be a major problem. So, the second way to achieve cost savings in transportation is to optimize the loading of trucks and containers, so that all the space is used up, and to pick the right packaging so as to minimize air between packages. Of course, minimizing packaging can be taken too far when it is not able to protect the product in transit. Finally, the manner in which products are handled in transit can be improved, by reducing the number of touchpoints and increasing the speed of execution. Sometimes, those savings can be achieved by implementing technology, but those decisions would have to be weighed against the upfront investment in that technology.

- **Human resources:** The supply chain management area of the company can be comprised of a large number of staff. While a significant number of people who work in manufacturing are likely to be earning an hourly wage (and therefore their costs would be part of the costs of goods sold category), the costs of employing salaried employees that cannot be tied to specific products are considered in this category. Regardless, if a company is able to reduce the number of people it employs, it not only saves the direct costs of employment but also the indirect costs that arise as a result of having those employees, such as human resource management costs. Not only do the employees need to be onboarded and trained on a continuous basis, but their employment likely carries other costs such as benefits and the like.
- **Information technology:** As previously mentioned in the beginning of this book, there are three primary flows in the supply chain: products, information, and finances. There is a significant information technology (IT) infrastructure that is associated with the supply chain. Often companies look to IT to provide solutions that fix supply chain issues. It can be argued that an efficient and effective supply chain diminishes the need to fix issues through IT, which in turn means that IT resources can be reduced or deployed elsewhere. Similarly, if supply chain processes are effective and well designed, then the deployment of IT is much easier. For example, when companies started implementing enterprise resource planning systems (ERP), processes needed to be mapped in the system. If those processes were not well established following best practices, either significant customization of the software

was required, which was very expensive, or processes needed to be changed to match the process prescribed by the system.

- **Finance/accounting:** Going back to the three primary flows, effective supply chain management can enable the firm to shift away finance and accounting resources from the operational side of the business. This means that there is less time spent on activities such as "chasing money," processing refunds, or other activities that would have been necessary due to supply chain errors. In addition, if the company is able to generate supply chain capital as described in the earlier chapters, the finance function would need to spend less time raising capital, which again reduces the need for those resources or frees them up to focus on other activities.

- **Research and development (R&D):** Lastly, there is a significant opportunity for supply chain management to impact research and development. A significant part of R&D has to do with bringing products to market. Because the rollout of products requires a great deal of advance procurement, production, and logistics costs, if SCM can play a prudent role in that early phase of a product's lifecycle, significant mistakes can be avoided and cost savings can be obtained. Similarly, even at the product design stage, procurement can have a positive influence on the actual development process by managing a supplier portfolio that is ready to be deployed. This reduces the need for R&D staff to search for suitable suppliers. Finally, if a company can integrate its suppliers into the development process, R&D costs can be shared across multiple companies.

In summary, as shown here, most companies have significant interrelations between the different functional areas of the firm and if one area is able to be more efficient, then it has positive outcomes for the whole firm (Table 4).

Balance Sheet

In addition to the impact of SCM on the income statement, there are several areas in which benefits on the balance sheet can be achieved.

Assets are defined as a tangible item of value that is held by a company. There are two types of assets, current assets, and non-current assets. Current assets are able to be converted into cash within the fiscal year, while non-current assets are those that the company plans to keep for longer periods of time than the fiscal year. Examples of current assets are cash and cash equivalents, receivables, and inventories. Non-current, or long-term assets are generally regarded as plants, property, and equipment. The assets of a company must balance with its liabilities plus shareholder equity. In other words, liabilities and equity must be balanced by assets. Liabilities are classified into two categories, current and long-term liabilities, based on when the company expects to pay them back (within the current fiscal year or later). An overview of the balance sheet items affected by supply chain management is shown in Table 5.

Table 5:   Impact of SCM on Balance Sheet

Assets	
Cash and Cash Equivalents	• Utilize supply chain capabilities to create supply chain capital • Reduce the need to generate cash through other means
Accounts Receivables	• Reduce accounts receivables through quicker payment
Inventories	• Improve forecasting and demand planning to reduce safety stock • Reduce raw material inventory through better procurement • Reduce WIP inventory through better manufacturing planning • Reduce finished goods inventory • Reduce obsolete inventory
PP&E	• Optimize capacity planning • Optimize equipment utilization • Improve plant and warehouse utilization and rationalization • Reduce assets through outsourcing
Liabilities	
Accounts Payables	• Lengthen payment terms to hold on to cash longer • Utilize SCF techniques to improve supplier accounts receivables and inventories while keeping cash as long as possible

Cash and Cash Equivalents

When a company is able to manage its supply chain capabilities more efficiently, its ability to generate supply chain capital is increased. For a more detailed discussion of supply chain capital, please refer to Chapter 4. This supply chain capital can be used to improve the company's cash reserves. Even if the company does not need to increase its cash reserves, there are a number of benefits that can be accomplished through the creation of supply chain capital. One example is the reduced need for the revolving line of credit with a bank. Those short-term loans cost the company interest and have other limiting factors, so the less reliant on the outside capital a firm can be, the better.

Accounts Receivables

When a company has fulfilled an order for a customer but it has yet to be paid for, that transaction is summarized in accounts receivables. On the flipside, the customer books that charge in accounts payables. This type of current asset is driven by supply chain activity. Using SCF tools, payments from customer to supplier can be accelerated, which deceases accounts receivables for the supplier and in turn increases cash. Accounts receivables can also be impacted by supply chain execution, as it is easier to convince customers to pay their invoices quicker if the company provides superior value. On the other hand, if a company fulfills orders late and its products are of inferior quality, then it could give customers an incentive to lengthen their payments until those issues are resolved or to target these suppliers for longer payment terms altogether.

Inventories

A company's inventory comes in a number of types, which are sometimes detailed on a firm's balance sheet, but the exact finance equivalent that is attributed to inventory is dependent on a number of factors. One major driver of inventory is the accuracy of demand planning, which in turn directly affects the need for safety stock. For example, if a company is able to forecast its demand better, its forecast error is less, which in turn means that threats of stocking out will be diminished and the need for high safety stocks are reduced. Similarly, procurement has an impact on how raw materials are delivered to the company's manufacturing facilities. This can impact the level of raw materials inventory that the company needs to hold. For example, some companies are able to reduce their raw materials inventory by asking their suppliers to move their operations to closer proximity. This is often the case with automotive manufacturing plants. Within manufacturing, lean production systems rely on very little work-in-process (WIP) inventory. But even in traditional manufacturing environments, there is less need for WIP if the production system is efficient and well managed. Lastly, within logistics, there is typically a large push to reduce inventory, as inventory efficiency is often one of the function's main performance metrics. The logistics function generally controls finished goods inventory and often is incentivized to keep inventory as low as possible, while maintaining service levels. Further reductions in finished goods inventory is often possible for obsolete inventory, which has lost its initial value. Sometimes called "dead stock," this inventory is no longer sought after by customers and therefore steps must be taken to move it quickly. In fact, for most companies, the best way to manage inventory is to increase the velocity of inventory and sell it as quickly as possible. If a product does not sell to the expectations of the firm, then alternative distribution channels might improve the speed at which the product sells.

Plant, Property, and Equipment (PP&E)

For manufacturing companies, the PP&E category of the balance sheet is largely comprised of supply chain assets. In addition to manufacturing operations some companies also maintain a network of logistics facilities, such as distribution centers, transportation terminals, and others. Those assets can make a company "asset-heavy" which is often seen as inefficient by investors. This can lead to a push to shed some of these assets by outsourcing functions that would be performed in-house. The most likely assets to be outsourced would be those related to logistics operations such as warehousing and transportation, but often companies consider moving manufacturing out as well to further improve their footprint. The basic idea is that companies that can achieve higher returns with fewer assets are more efficient and valuable.

Accounts Payables

On the liability side of the balance sheet, supply chain management (and especially procurement) controls the interactions with suppliers. While traditionally, the standard metric for most procurement professionals has been cost reduction, they have influence over payment terms (as discussed earlier) and therefore directly affect accounts payables. While still a liability, when a company extends payables, the increase is also accompanied by an increase in cash, so there is a significant benefit for the financial standing of the firm. This realization is fundamental to practicing SCF activities.

Chapter 10

Conclusions

Purchasing and Supply Chain Financing

Our goal has been to develop a deeper understanding of supply chain financing (SCF) and the analytical tools that facilitate SCF. We have gathered our information from interviewing professionals and studying documentation from a select group of CAPS Research member companies. We have also collected information from major banks, non-traditional lenders, and newly established and more established fintech companies. We hope this book provides ideas and tools that procurement professionals can utilize to improve the financial positions of their firms.

For many firms, their greatest challenge is maintaining a strong cash flow. A large percentage of the senior management of companies is focused on working capital management. It is clear Wall Street expects that firms will maintain a clean balance sheet and carefully manage working capital. Despite a general easing in most credit markets in the United States, many non-investment-grade companies and smaller enterprises have found it difficult to finance their working capital requirements. These firms make up a large portion of the supply base for larger companies that have substantially better access to capital. Consequently, there is a significant credit arbitrage difference between large companies and their supply bases. SCF programs can assist these buying firms to monetize this arbitrage opportunity while helping their supply bases.

Global business has grown more complex and the knowledge and skills that procurement professionals need to have has increased dramatically. Good supply management includes managing the balance sheet of the firm and carefully managing costs. While achieving purchasing savings is important and is likely to be rewarded inside a procurement organization, understanding the impact of working capital and its role in a firm is important. For procurement organizations, understanding the financial variables becomes imperative to keep a company vibrant.

Procurement should have a seat at the table, especially concerning the issues around SCF. They should work with the treasury and finance functions regarding working capital management and understand how the market value of the firm is impacted by the amount of cash available. Firms are being measured on their cash conversion cycles (CCCs), which is a measure of their management of working capital. For instance, Apple manages its cash flows masterfully with one of the best CCCs, and it is not accidental that it is such a valuable firm.[1] While its products are innovative and generally have good margins, the financial management side of the company has accumulated very large amounts of cash to greatly improve the market value of the company. For some firms, CCC is actually a metric that is used to evaluate supply chain performance. In whatever manner companies utilize CCC, it is clear that unlocking working capital is critical.

It should also be highlighted that CPOs generally impact two of three components in the CCC, which are inventories and accounts payable. In some cases, they may even influence the third and final component of CCC, which is accounts receivables, by contributing to revenue generation.

Pressures on Inventories, Payables, and Receivables

Supply chain management professionals often are under pressure to tighten inventories as much as possible. Getting better inventory

---

[1] Graham, J. and Smart, S. B. (2011). "Cash Conversion, Inventory, and Receivables Management." *Introduction to Corporate Finance: What Companies Do*, Third Edition, Cengage Learning, Boston, MA.

performance has enabled companies to decrease costs while at the same time build in agility. Increasingly, supply chain organizations are being asked to help manage receivables and payables. In consequence, purchasing managers are asking their suppliers to extend their payables terms. Over the last few years, it has become standard in several industries to greatly increase the length of the firm's accounts payables terms. In the consumer packaged goods industry, several leading companies, including Procter & Gamble and Kellogg's, have moved their payables terms to 120 days.[2] In the automobile parts retail sector, many companies begin negotiating with suppliers for payables terms of one year.

While it is possible to simply lengthen payment terms, such as what some companies have done, this often comes at a great strain to suppliers.[3] To make themselves whole, some suppliers will raise prices or build defensive language into the contracts. And, as mentioned earlier, several are turning to banks or fintech companies to help maintain a better cash position. Some attempt to shorten the time for the accounts receivable cycle. Since these attempts are happening at the exact same time when buying firms are working to extend their payables, they create tension between the buying firm and suppliers. Often, a supplier's attempts are not successful because the buying firm has more negotiating power. We consider efficient SCF programs to be able to lessen the negative impact on the suppliers.

The Next Frontier

Supply chain financing is the next frontier of supply management. According to one expert, it is estimated that penetration of SCF programs is around 5 percent. There are several reasons for the slow diffusion of SCF as an innovation. One key reason may be the lack of realizing the

[2] Storm, S. (2015). "Big Companies Pay Later, Squeezing Their Suppliers." *The New York Times*. Retrieved from www.nytimes.com/2015/04/07/business/big-companies-pay-later-squeezing-their-suppliers.html.
[3] Buck, G. (2016). "Boeing Puts Squeeze on Suppliers." *The Global Treasurer*. Retrieved from www.theglobaltreasurer.com/2016/07/11/boeing-puts-squeeze-on-suppliers/.

importance of improving working capital and using a firm's strong balance sheet to solidify its position in the supply chain.

In many firms, supply management professionals are called upon to help fund the growth of the firm. It is also likely that companies will use their financial strength to assist developing suppliers to become better, more viable companies. Fundamentally, SCF is about improving buyer–supplier relationships. Therefore, the job of managing of cash and funding does not just belong to the finance area. Purchasing should play an integral role in designing, implementing, and maintaining SCF.

We are still in the early stages of SCF innovation. There already is a wide variety of SCF service offerings available, but it is likely that new types of service firms will develop over the next few years. SCF is an area that is ripe for creative new firms to help make the supply chain function better. It is likely that in the next 10 years there will be new types of firms in the area of SCF that we cannot imagine at present. SCF is both an area where we can expect great change and important results. The financial flows both inside and outside the firm should be the key consideration in designing the supply chain. The financial flows and relationships therein can determine supply chain variables such as facility location, currency exchange, contracting, and numerous other elements. Firms will continue to look to their supply chains to finance their organizations and vice versa.

Appendix A

Fees for Card Transactions

For firms using the card interchange network, a fee is applied to each transaction. The transmitters have a variety of different interchange rates. There is a standard B2B transaction rate, which is referred to by the commercial card companies as Level 1 data. The levels correlate with the size of the fee that is charged with the interchange. There are also what are known as incentive interchange rates, where lower rates are applied to a given number of data points captured in each transaction, which are called Level 2 and Level 3. For example, if the merchant provides enhanced data such as sales tax and a unique customer code, that would be considered Level 2 data. The final data level, Level 3, would include invoice level data such as order date, invoice number, SKU information, and address verification.

Rates get significantly lower for the merchant if Level 3 information is provided. These types of data can provide significant value to the buying organization, especially in an environment where cards are distributed throughout the organization. All that information, once consolidated, can be used to more effectively manage spending within the organization.

A different rate independent from the previously described levels applies to high-value transactions. This information is shown in Figure A.1, which compares Level 3 transactions, which are transferred at

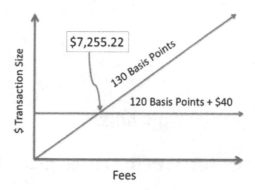

Figure A.1:   High Ticket Transactions versus Level 3 Transactions

a fixed 130 BP, with high-value transactions which are transferred at a fixed $40 plus 120 BP. The point where the two lines cross, at $7,255.22, is the break-even point.

Appendix B

SupplierPay Initiative

SupplierPay was an initiative driven by President Barack Obama to help small- and medium-sized firms get paid earlier by their customer firms. Subsequently, the program moved to the Small Business Administration, which still manages it. A similar program in the United Kingdom titled the Prompt Payment Code (PPC) preceded the US version, which kicked off in 2014. The PPC in the United Kingdom sets standards for payment practices. The Chartered Institute of Credit Management administers the PPC.

The White House recognized that lengthening payment terms has had detrimental effects on smaller suppliers with limited access to liquidity. The White House urged large corporations to sign on to its voluntary SupplierPay initiative.[1] The initiative resembles the federal government's own QuickPay program that was started in 2011 and attempts to pay small business suppliers within 15 days. In a statement, the White House claims that the QuickPay initiative has raised more than $1 billion for small business since its inception. There are numerous companies that have signed on to support the pledge. A major influential factor for this initiative is positive publicity. When coupled with the recent negative press that some firms have received as a result of their longer payment terms, this is an

---

[1]The White House (2014). Retrieved from www.whitehouse.gov/the-press-office/2014/07/11/president-obama-announces-new-partnership-private-sector-strengthen-amer.

issue that requires significant attention.[2] It requires significant alignment and collaboration with leaders in the finance area. The UK version (PPC) includes compliance monitoring. Principles of the Code are monitored and enforced by the PPC Compliance Board. The Code covers prompt payment, as well as wider payment procedures. The US version of the SupplierPay pledge is presented below.

SupplierPay Pledge

Strengthening small business access to capital is a "win–win" for small companies and us, their large customers. We recognize that we thrive when supply chains are healthy, when firms of all sizes are able to support our growth, investing in new ideas and new equipment, and creating new jobs. We do best when Main Street is strong, as small businesses are critical to our reaching our full economic potential as a company and a nation. Small firms are responsible for the majority of US job creation and generate close to half of the US gross domestic product. While small firms have made momentous strides in recovering from the depths of the Great Recession, too many small businesses continue to struggle to access capital, including working capital, which creates a drag on growth and employment.

We are committed to addressing this marketplace gap in small business lending. Our efforts are intended as a meaningful step in reinvigorating our supply chains, making them more resilient over time while supporting Main Street today. Accordingly we resolve to do the following:

1. *Provide a Working Capital Solution to Our Small Business Suppliers*: We will take active steps to lower the working capital cost of small business suppliers through either of the following:
    *   Paying our small suppliers faster than we do today in order to reduce their capital needs.

---

[2]Ng, Serena (2013). "P&G, Big Companies Pinch Suppliers on Payments." *The Wall Street Journal*. Retrieved from http://www.wsj.com/articles/SB10001424127887324010704578418 361635041842.

- Enabling a financing solution that helps small suppliers to access working capital at a lower cost.

2. *Share Best Practices*: Our pledge is a first step in a larger effort to strengthen supply chains and support small firms with the goal of driving impactful follow-on action from the broader marketplace. To encourage wider support, we'll highlight tangible outcomes for our own efforts, providing visibility into our actions and publicize key learnings in implementing this pledge.

3. *Implement a "Win–Win" Solution*: We will implement this pledge in a manner that ensures our small suppliers are able to take advantage of our commitment while minimizing new administrative or operational burdens. We will define "small supplier," and if we choose to offer these solutions to the entire supply chain we will continue to focus our efforts on the small suppliers that will benefit most. We will not use our pledge to offer financing solutions as a means of extending payment terms with our current small business supplier base.

Appendix C

Supply Chain Finance at BPC (Case Study)*

This case study incorporates the concepts and illustrations discussed in this book. Its purpose is to capture them in a real-world user case. Professionals can treat this case as a capstone experience where different concepts come together. A reader may also use this case for training purposes. The motivation behind this case study is to highlight a situation in which the company may consider using the SCF tools and concepts covered in this book. The time period in which this case is set is 2015.

Introduction

Adam Clayton retreated to his private study in the CEO suite at Big Pharma Corporation (BPC) and asked his assistant to hold all calls. He began slowly thinking through the events of the last few years...

BPC had undergone a major transformation since Clayton had been selected by the Board of Directors to move from his role as chief financial officer (CFO) to become the new CEO. Not only had the executive team experienced a major reorganization, but a new mind-set was institutionalized that was much more focused on financial efficiency and results. Recently, it was really proving difficult to drive the kind of change the

---

*The authors would like to thank Eric Larson for his contributions to earlier versions of this case study.

Board of Directors was expecting, and it was time to take stock of his position. As CFO, he had been eager to find ways to finance the growth initiatives from 2005 to 2013; but now, BPC was highly leveraged, and new debt was not really possible without alarming the capital markets. Along the same lines, the company's working capital, which he had fought so hard in the past to improve, was under pressure. Namely, the cash conversion cycle (CCC) he achieved three years ago, had been stalled at around the same level since it peaked in 2014, and it was far from best in class.

Market dynamics, and the traditional forces that influenced the overall competitiveness of the pharmaceutical industry, were all moving the wrong way. Clayton saw increasing pricing pressures coming not only from foreign healthcare systems negotiating better but also from US organizations, such as the increasingly coordinated group purchasing organizations (GPO), healthcare exchanges, and Tricare/Medicare. Some mainline BPC products, which had contributed large profits for many years, were facing the loss of exclusivity, and would soon be challenged by generics. Clayton witnessed several of his competitors tightening their supply chains by consolidating their plant capacities, using more subcontractors across their supply chains, or performing "reverse mergers" (where a larger US company merges itself into a smaller European company to achieve the lower effective tax rate associated with the new European headquarters). Sales and R&D productivity had not grown in years, and upstart "bioPharmas" were hurdling barriers to entry quickly by developing single, but significant, "indications" (i.e., drugs to treat a particular condition) for cancer that BPC also wanted to develop. It was indeed, a tough time for Clayton to be increasing his earnings to the level that the Board expected.

As Clayton reviewed his situation, his main concern centered on the fact that BPC needed products that would power the company's growth and cash flow for years to come. There were several ways to achieve the desired growth; the two which were most prominent were (1) to invest greater sums in BPC's own R&D or (2) to acquire/merge with companies that had successful indications. Either way, BPC was going to need better access to capital to fund those kinds of investments. During the early years of Adam Clayton's tenure as CFO, supply chain management had achieved some fairly impressive improvements in its cash conversion cycle, which had released an important level of working capital. However, the past months' events had been very difficult for Clayton, and he especially loathed to lose further ground due solely to arm-twisting from the US White House.

The SupplierPay initiative, launched by the President of the United States, has recently been introduced to promote and enhance the financial environment for small- and medium-sized businesses. Larger manufacturers, like BPC, were invited to the White House to discuss the initiative and encouraged, in front of their peers and the President, to sign a pledge to treat smaller suppliers better by paying them more quickly. While this initiative did not have the force of law, Clayton chose to sign the agreement, in part due to the encouragement of his fellow CEOs and the fact that one of BPC's biggest customers is the US government (Medicare). The pledge posed a rather large challenge: should BPC actually follow through on this pledge, and lose significant working capital? Might there potentially be a way to implement the program very slowly, and at least retain the current benchmarked position, or could BPC robustly follow through on the pledge, but replace the lost working capital from other sources? Clayton leaned back in his executive chair, drew a deep breath, and started to think about all of the issues which impacted his capital.

The Pharmaceutical Sector

Pharmaceuticals are a mature sector within the broader healthcare industry. It is expected that growth for the next 10 years is at about, or slightly below, the rate of the overall economy. Traditionally, pharmaceuticals have been one of the most profitable sectors in the US economy. Yet, in the past years, profitability has generally grown due to raising prices, lowering costs, devising more efficient methods for R&D, and exploiting economies of scale via mergers and acquisitions (M&A). Some companies have recently been leveraging reverse mergers for lower effective tax rates.

Historically, the pharmaceutical sector has relied upon improvements in technology to discover potential new products. Lately, the pace of new drug discovery from R&D has slowed considerably, while the cost of that work has risen dramatically. The development and commercialization of so-called "blockbuster drugs" has been slowing, making it increasingly challenging for the more R&D-intensive companies to recover their costs with products that in the past earned several billion dollars. Subsequently, the focus of R&D efforts is shifting to products that are less lucrative or niche products. In addition, more rigorous government regulations, amplified scrutiny, and increased safety concerns have also impacted the productivity of pharmaceutical R&D operations.

Over the past decade, an increasing number of key drugs lost their patent protection, heightening competitive pressures from generic products. On the customer side, the healthcare sector is also consolidating, increasing the bargaining power of customers. Together, these trends have limited industry growth and initiated a period of change. For these reasons, many firms have turned to M&A to increase efficiency. Three examples of "mega-mergers" in 2009 were Pfizer acquiring Wyeth, Merck acquiring Schering-Plough, and Roche acquiring the part of Genentech that it did not already own.

Pharmaceutical market and product categories include preparations, medicinal and botanical products, biologics, and *in vitro* diagnostic products, while the industry's products are typically broken down into treatment areas. The top five areas are oncology, diabetes, mental health, respiratory, and pain treatment which are explained as follows:

- Oncology is expected to make up 10.8 percent of overall sales. According to the American Cancer Society, 1.6 million new cancer cases are expected to occur in the United States in 2015. High cancer drug prices have restricted patients' access and, according to a 2013 study, (Oncologist Express) between 10 percent and 20 percent of cancer patients forego treatment due to costs. It is expected that more stringent oncology drug pricing regulations will limit the extent to which firms can maintain high prices.
- Diabetes drugs are expected to make up 9.4 percent of overall sales. The Centers for Disease Control and Prevention (CDC) estimates that the number of diabetic individuals rose from 21.1 million to 22.3 million between 2010 and 2013. Hence, it is no surprise that over the past years, demand for anti-diabetic drugs has risen.

- According to the Pharmaceutical Research and Manufacturers of America (PhRMA), pharmaceutical companies have increasingly focused their R&D on mental health drugs, to focus on the 61.5 million Americans who have mental health disorders. Currently, the share of mental health drugs is 9.2 percent of sales.
- According to the American Lung Association, asthma is the most common chronic disease, affecting about 40 million people in the United States. Over the past years, the respiratory segment has remained stable at around 7.9 percent of overall sales.
- Lastly, the pain treatment category provides a stable prescription and over-the-counter customer base of 7.2 percent of sales.

Background on BPC

BPC is a major player in the pharmaceutical industry, manufacturing both traditional, small-molecule pharmaceutical products, as well as the latest immunotherapeutic drugs, part of the segment called biopharmaceuticals. The corporation as a whole is engaged in the discovery, development, licensing, manufacturing, marketing, distribution, and sale of pharmaceutical products. Most industry experts consider BPC one of the top five global players in the industry. Its products are sold to wholesalers, retail pharmacies, hospitals, and government agencies across the world. The company manufactures its products in the United States, Puerto Rico, and six additional foreign countries.

BPC's executive team is made up of CEO Adam Clayton and six senior officers of the company, responsible for finance, marketing, information technologies, product development, research, and supply chain management (see Figure C.1). Widely considered as the most influential member of the team, Beth Moore has Clayton's former job as the CFO. As a result, the strategic direction of the firm is geared toward financial excellence. To deliver on this imperative, Moore, who is overseeing the traditional finance function, also has staff reporting to her that are embedded in each one of the other previously mentioned functional areas. One area that has recently been elevated is supply chain management. Previously just a cost center and managed by the specific product teams

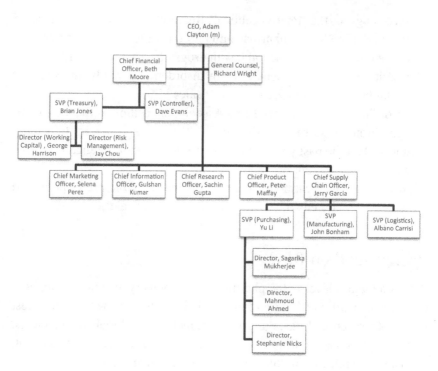

Figure C.1:   BPC Organizational Chart

in a decentralized manner, supply chain is now deemed critical to success. In fact, the Board of Directors and the CEO both recognized a few years ago that execution of the go-to-market strategy, after drugs had been developed, was critical to making any kind of progress in this newly competitive industry.

To build the corporate SCM group, BPC hired Jerry Garcia, who spent his prior career in the consumer packaged goods industry. He was highly familiar, from his years at Colgate-Palmolive, with the expectation that SCM be responsible for helping to improve the financial standing of the firm. The other functional heads were not used to this structure and therefore come to Garcia for advice. Overall, he is a well-respected member of the executive leadership team who has built enough social capital to occasionally ask for a favor.

The Cash Conversion Cycle as a Supply Chain Measure

Clayton believed that the financial efficiency in the pharma industry was lagging severely behind more financially savvy industries, such as electronics, where he had spent most of his career prior to coming to BPC. The goal was to exert even tighter control over the available capital and expenses. Working capital is of major concern to the leadership of the firm, not just because it is a significant concern for Wall Street analysts but also because this capital is needed to drive R&D investment. As such, Jerry Garcia is measured not only on traditional supply chain goals, such as predictability and responsiveness, but also the impact that SCM had on the P&L, balance sheet, and cash flow (see Figure C.2).

The fact that Garcia is responsible for achieving superior service at a competitive cost was not new in the industry. However, one of the most important balance sheet metrics is the CCC or cash conversion cycle. It is affected by the supply chain organization in three ways: accounts payable, inventory, and accounts receivable (see Table C.1).

Customer Satisfaction	Financial Performance
Predictability "Make promises and keep them" • On-time delivery of BPC and suppliers • Fill rate / Service level • Forecast and Inventory accuracy	**Profit and Loss Statement** "Deliver world-class cost structure" • Gross margin return on investment • Total Supply Chain Costs as % of revenue • Y/Y contribution to profits
Responsiveness "Provide quick and flexible supply" • Order fulfillment lead time • Supplier flexibility • Multiple seamless delivery options	**Balance Sheet and Cash Flow** "Maintain high velocity in assets" • Cash Conversion Cycle (CCC) • Net asset turns • Customer days of supply

Figure C.2: Supply Chain Management Performance Chart

Table C.1:   Cash Conversion Cycle

Metric	Description	Calculation
Cash Conversion Cycle (CCC)	A metric describing how efficiently the firm can generate cash.	CCC = DSO + DIO – DPO
Days Sales Outstanding (DSO)	The number of days needed to collect on sales.	DSO = accounts receivable/daily sales
Days Inventory Outstanding (DIO)	How many days it takes to sell the available inventory.	DIO = inventory/daily COGS
Days Payable Outstanding (DPO)	The company's payment of its own bills.	DPO = accounts payable/daily COGS

The CCC is an important metric that connects the firm to its customers and suppliers. It is made up of days sales outstanding (DSO), days payable outstanding (DPO), and days inventory outstanding (DIO). It is a meaningful measure especially for firms that have physical goods, such as BPC. It has gained acceptance and preference not only among finance and treasury executives, but it also impacts the supply chain domain and therefore is increasingly used to measure supply chain performance. The CCC is directly tied to the working capital needs of the firm, which is why it is often used by analysts to evaluate the ability of the firm to efficiently manage cash. Conceptually, the CCC measures the time associated with operating the business — the time between the outflow of cash for needed materials and services and the inflow of cash from customers who buy products. In other words, a lower value for CCC is better than a higher value because a lower CCC represents that a firm is converting work into cash more quickly. Overall, the CCC has improved over time for BPC (see Table C.2).

After performing a benchmarking analysis of BPC and its closest competitors, it was clear that BPC needed to implement some changes (see Table C.3). While it was not at the bottom of the industry, one competitor (Bristol-Myers-Squibb) in particular was leaps ahead and BPC had stopped closing the gap. This situation was not acceptable to Clayton or Moore, and they made it very clear that Garcia had to address this gap.

Table C.2: BPC's Cash Conversion Cycle

Year Ending	DSO	DPO	DIO	CCC
2015	56	113	136	79
2014	54	122	131	63
2013	60	102	129	87
2012	68	93	145	120
2011	77	64	166	179
2010	88	39	188	237

Table C.3: Cash Conversion Cycle Benchmarking Study

	DSO Comparison	DPO Comparison	DIO Comparison	Cash Conversion Cycle
BPC	56	113	136	79
Amgen, Inc.	52	100	218	166
Bristol-Myers-Squibb Co.	66	231	145	−20
J&J	54	122	131	63
Merck & Co Inc.	57	57	121	121
Pfizer	64	122	216	208
Pharma and Biotech Sector	60	93	145	112
Healthcare Industry	44	49	54	49

While BPC was not in terrible shape, there were two areas where BPC could focus its improvements efforts: DIO and DPO. Compared with other industries, inventory turns are significantly lower and industry experts believe there are significant improvements possible.[3] While DPO

---

[3] Outlook on Pharma Operations, by David Keeling, Martin Lösch, Ulf Schrader, www.mckinsey.com/~/media/mckinsey/dotcom/client_service/operations/pdfs/outlook_on_pharma_operations.ashx.

performance is significantly better in pharma than in other industries, the longer payment terms are correlated to the higher inventory that is typical for the pharma sector. In other words, in most industries, companies strive for DPO to be about equal to DIO, but it is not unusual to have DPO be much larger than DIO for the top-performing pharmaceutical firms.

The SupplierPay Initiative

The White House recently brought attention to the fact that the largest corporations in the United States have lengthened their payment terms, from an industry standard of 30 days with a 2 percent discount for early payments within 10 days (2/10 net 30), to much longer payment terms. This practice had significant negative effects on smaller companies, especially small businesses and diverse suppliers. Therefore, the President invited the CEOs from several of the largest US companies to the White House and asked them to sign a pledge to pay small businesses much faster. While some companies showed some tepid developments, others quickly embraced the program.[4] The concern at BPC was that larger suppliers would not accept the already-long payment terms if they realized that smaller suppliers got paid much faster. If this pledge were implemented without any other considerations, the CCC would quickly rise to levels not seen for several years and, in turn, seriously affect not just the performance metric for Jerry Garcia but also the entire finance organization.

Supplier Management at BPC

The suppliers to BPC have traditionally been categorized into four distinct categories: Strategic, Leverage, Bottleneck, and Routine. This categorization is shown as a two-by-two matrix with supply risk and potential to add value as the axes (see Figure C.3). Strategic suppliers make up a majority of the total spend with about 40 percent share, while representing roughly

---

[4]www.pymnts.com/in-depth/2014/supplierpay-initiative-pushes-large-companies-to-speed-payments-to-smbs/.

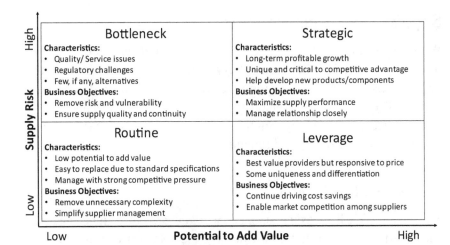

	Bottleneck	Strategic
High	**Characteristics:** • Quality/ Service issues • Regulatory challenges • Few, if any, alternatives **Business Objectives:** • Remove risk and vulnerability • Ensure supply quality and continuity	**Characteristics:** • Long-term profitable growth • Unique and critical to competitive advantage • Help develop new products/components **Business Objectives:** • Maximize supply performance • Manage relationship closely
Supply Risk	Routine	Leverage
Low	**Characteristics:** • Low potential to add value • Easy to replace due to standard specifications • Manage with strong competitive pressure **Business Objectives:** • Remove unnecessary complexity • Simplify supplier management	**Characteristics:** • Best value providers but responsive to price • Some uniqueness and differentiation **Business Objectives:** • Continue driving cost savings • Enable market competition among suppliers
	Low **Potential to Add Value** High	

Figure C.3:   Supplier Management Strategic Map

5 percent of the number of suppliers. The Leverage category accounts for 30 percent of the total spend and approximately 30 percent of the accounts. The Bottleneck category accounts for 10 percent of the total spend and around 20 percent of the number of accounts. Finally, the Routine category makes up about 20 percent of the total spend while representing around 45 percent of the accounts. The specific management of the relationships with the supplier categories falls upon the purchasing and supply management organization, which reports to Jerry Garcia and is headed up by Yu Li, a senior vice president at BPC. She also manages the relationships with the strategic suppliers directly, while some of the most critical strategic suppliers have access to Garcia as well. The other three categories, Bottleneck, Leverage, and Routine are managed by the three directors reporting to Li, Sagarika Mukherjee, Mahmoud Ahmed, and Stephanie Nicks, respectively.

This categorization did not take into account or give any clue as to which suppliers were affected by the SupplierPay initiative, such as smaller companies and minority-owned businesses. After conducting an internal study, it was determined that most of the smaller companies were in the Routine category and a few are considered Bottleneck suppliers.

Supply Chain Finance Tools

With the benchmarked "gap" in CCC clearly in mind, and needing it to be resolved quickly, Beth Moore and Jerry Garcia had asked their respective teams to research the potential tools that could be used to address the issue at hand. The teams met continuously over a short period and came up with three possibly overlapping solutions: commercial credit cards, supply chain finance, and dynamic discounts.

Commercial Credit Cards

Many firms have been using commercial credit cards for purchasing travel and entertainment. Over the last decade, the focus of commercial card programs has turned increasingly to applications in procurement. The US federal government has been a proponent of commercial cards. It has developed a program called SmartPay that routes about $30 billion in spending annually onto cards.[5] MasterCard and Visa anchor the program and are joined by three banks: US Bank, Citigroup, and JPMorgan Chase.

There are three major benefits to using commercial cards. First, finance executives appreciate how they can simplify the administrative side of payments, especially payments to small, niche suppliers. The cost of processing an invoice is estimated to be around $75, while the cost of processing a purchase order is estimated to be around $250. Given the average value of a credit card transaction is about $4, the relatively low administrative overhead associated with commercial cards is one of the biggest advantages. Second, cards can provide some DPO advantage, as the default payment term is typically 45 days and can be extended further if needed. In most industries, the use of cards does not present a difference to the current DPO.

The last advantage of cards is that there are the benefits of rebates on the purchases. There are varying rebate fee structures depending on annual spend volume. These rebates are negotiated between the issuer and the firm when a card program is established. These rebates can range from 0.5 percent to 1.5 percent depending on the total volume of the annual

---

[5] https://smartpay.gsa.gov/.

transactions. The major barrier to wider adoption of cards is the rather high fees, which are between 2.5 percent and 4 percent, that are charged to sellers. There are some new fintech companies that seem to be breaking out of that traditional system, but the overwhelming majority of card transactions are made via the traditional interchange networks, such as American Express, MasterCard, or Visa.[6]

Supply Chain Finance Programs

A key product offered by many large banks to their business customers is trade finance. Often, supply chain finance programs are part of global trade finance and their treasury management solutions.[7] These programs can be used to ensure payment and reduce risk in global transactions. This financial service was previously known as *reverse factoring*. There are several ways a firm can implement a program, but at its core, suppliers receive the option to obtain early payment for a small fee that is calculated based on the buyer's credit risk.

The basic notion of supply chain finance programs is that buyers are able to pay their suppliers with specific terms (e.g., in 180 days), while allowing the supplier to receive early payments (e.g., as early as 12 days after invoice submission). A typical arrangement is shown in Figure C.4. Solid lines indicate movement of money or goods, while broken lines reflect facilitating activities such as agreements. Generally, payments are routed through the SCF provider. The provider will then manage the relationship with the funders, who often are banks but can also be insurance companies, mutual funds, or retirement funds. It is also the provider who has the direct financing relationship with the supplier. It is important that the buyer is outside the day-to-day decisions of the provider. If the supplier agrees to the arrangement, it receives early payment, at a discounted rate that is based on the buyer's credit. It basically enjoys short-term liquidity at a favorable rate. It is a risk premium on top of a standard

---

[6]http://spendmatters.com/tfmatters/when-jpmorgan-or-citibank-and-oxygen-finance-or-taulia-knock-on-the-same-corporate-door/.

[7]http://spendmatters.com/tfmatters/5-reasons-why-banks-will-win-the-trade-financing-and-p2p-game-someday/.

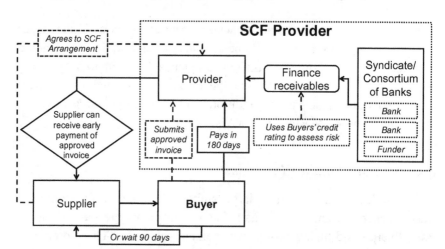

Figure C.4:   Supply Chain Finance Process

interest charge, such as the London Interbank Offered Rate (LIBOR), which can range between 0.5 percent and 3.5 percent. For a company such as BPC, it would be at the lower end of the spectrum. This rate represents a significantly lower interest rate for a majority of suppliers than they would be able to obtain directly from a financial institution on their own credentials. It is thus generally viewed as an effective tool to provide cheap liquidity to a large firm's supply chain.

Fintechs

Fintechs, in the supply chain finance realm, are companies that utilize technology to reinvent financial systems and make funding the supply chain more efficient. They are *not* banks, but operate on technology platforms that use a funding source to connect with the buyer and supplier. In addition, they are not under the same regulations as banks and consequently are able to create more innovative practices.[8] These innovations have led to increased options for small- and medium-sized (SME) suppliers. In some cases, fintechs have developed new

---

[8] http://spendmatters.com/tfmatters/give-me-my-share-of-wallet-bankers-cry/.

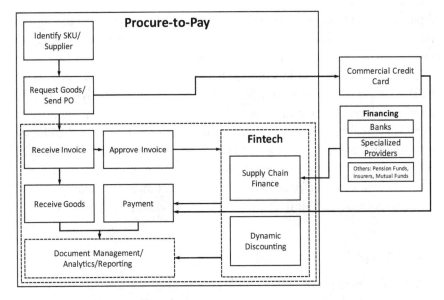

Figure C.5: Fintechs within the Procure-to-Pay Framework

procure-to-pay capabilities. In others, they have become a buying firm's purchasing system and include cataloging of suppliers (a database of approved suppliers), PO transmission, and electronic invoicing and payment. Figure C.5 shows how early payment of invoices is enabled and the integration with commercial credit card providers, or a connection with a number of funders that can finance receivables at competitive interest rates. Furthermore, some of these firms have the ability to provide dynamic discounting.

Dynamic Discounting

Dynamic discounting is a program where the supplier has the option to receive direct early payment from the buyer at a variable discount rate. For example, if a firm has a standard 2/10 net 30 term and it chooses to apply the same discount in a dynamic manner, then the daily interest would be 0.1 percent (20 days earlier payment in exchange for 2 percent). Therefore, if a supplier wanted to get paid 30 days early it would be charged a

3 percent discount. The downside of this tool is that the buyer has to use its own money, since it is a direct payment. If there is any financing involved, it could lead to accounting issues.

Another variation of this offered by one of the fintech companies (i.e., C2FO), applies an auction model to dynamic discounting, rather than a fixed structure. For example, if a buying firm has a certain amount of cash to disburse to its suppliers in exchange for additional discounts, then it can auction off those early payments. The platform will create a session akin to a reverse auction, where suppliers can bid for that early payment. So, for suppliers who need to accelerate collection of their outstanding receivables, they have the ability to join this auction via the online platform.

Next Steps

Adam Clayton expected a lot from his team. He knew that somehow they were expected to deliver the capital required. His team had to weigh whether a supply chain finance (SCF) program would be feasible and what the expected inflow of cash would be from the resulting payment term extension. In addition, would dynamic discounting and commercial cards be in the mix? If so, how would they decide which supplier was offered one of those options. They didn't just have to understand a number of new technologies, but more importantly, how the technologies could be used together to create the right strategy for BPC. This integration would be bound to affect a number of stakeholders who each viewed the issue through different lenses. While BPC was generally viewed as a strong company financially (see Table C.4), they could not rest on their past successes.

First and foremost, what would BPC's suppliers say to these initiatives? This effort was sure to affect not only the supply chain group, but specifically suppliers in the Strategic category. No matter what options BPC might select, it was going to be imperative that the strategy did not negatively affect relationships with the most critical suppliers.

Second, Clayton had always regarded working capital as a precious resource. No matter what the solution or mix of solutions, Clayton was keen to free up and maximize working capital. Both Chief Marketing Officer Selena Perez and Chief Research Officer Sachin Gupta have

Table C.4: BPC Financials: Income Statement

	2015	2014	2013
Sales to Customers	$31,430	$32,313	$28,125
Cost of Products Sold	$9,659	$9,888	$8,812
Gross Profit	**$21,771**	**$22,425**	**$19,313**
Selling, Marketing & Administrative Expenses	$9,510	$9,544	$8,610
Research & Development Expense	$4,057	$3,692	$3,227
In-process Research & Development Expense	$100	$77	$229
Interest Income	$57	$29	$29
Interest Expense, Net of Portion Capitalized	$248	$232	$190
Other Income (Expense), Net	$926	$30	−$985
Restructuring	$228	—	—
Earnings (Loss) before Taxes on Income — United States	$3,668	$3,478	$1,681
Earnings (Loss) before Taxes on Income — International	$4,941	$5,461	$4,421
Earnings before Provision for Taxes on Income	**$8,610**	**$8,939**	**$6,102**
Current United States Income Taxes Provision (Benefit)	$1,233	$1,141	$234
Current International Income Taxes Provision (Benefit)	$587	$510	$652
Total Current Income Taxes Provision (Benefit)	$1,820	$1,651	$886
Deferred United States Income Taxes Provision (Benefit)	$17	−$112	−$99
Deferred International Income Taxes Provision (Benefit)	−$138	$304	−$140
Total Deferred Income Taxes Provision (Benefit)	−$121	$192	−$239
Provision for Taxes on Income	$1,699	$1,843	$647
Net Earnings	**$6,911**	**$7,096**	**$5,455**

Note: All figures are in millions of dollars.

continuously expressed their concern that the continued pressure on their budgets was affecting their ability to consistently increase sales. As such, they were strongly supportive of any initiatives targeting working capital.

Third, Chief Information Officer Gulshan Kumar had concerns over the integration of any new systems into the existing IT infrastructure. Finally, BPC's controller was concerned about possible accounting implications that may cause supply chain finance transactions to be classified as loans rather than accounts payable.

With the future of BPC in mind, Clayton decided the success of the proposed program would be measured on the amount of working capital that could be generated. Specifically, cash on their balance sheet needed to be increased significantly (see Table C.5). While this would be driven by the technique ultimately chosen, the acceptance among suppliers would be key. Not only should the suppliers that are targeted with the program accept it, but they should also make use of the early pay option as often as possible, and ideally remain in the program for the foreseeable future. With that option, the SCF service provider must also be able to handle as many suppliers as possible. While capacity was certainly something to investigate, BPC has informally been told that it is an issue with some service providers. There was also talk, with respect to providers, that the ease of onboarding suppliers can be another source of differentiation. While the general question to the team was to devise a strategy detailing how working capital should be improved, in light of the SupplierPay pledge, it was also important for them to come up with at least a short list of preferred supply chain financing providers. Once this project is given the "green light," the team was sure that the solutions they would ultimately choose would have to be implemented quickly.

Clayton realized that the SupplierPay pledge could not have come at a worse time. BPC was currently in the midst of a secret negotiation to acquire an upstart cancer immunotherapy company that could potentially provide patent-protected profits for years to come. In his meetings with investment bankers regarding the acquisition, issuing new debt or equity had been ruled out — as such, the only option would be to self-fund the

Table C.5: **BPC Financials: Balance Sheet**

	2015	2014	2013
ASSETS			
Current Assets			
Cash & Cash Equivalents	$6,159	$6,313	$8,253
Marketable Securities	$11,053	$8,071	$3,265
Gross Accounts Receivable Trade	$4,935	$4,895	$4,751
Less Allowances for Doubtful Accounts	$120	$120	$131
Net Accounts Receivable Trade	$4,814	$4,775	$4,620
Inventories			
Raw Materials & Supplies	$420	$528	$483
Goods in Process	$1,005	$1,070	$1,030
Finished Goods	$2,187	$1,960	$1,594
Total Inventories	**$3,612**	**$3,558**	**$3,107**
Deferred Taxes on Income	—	$1,551	$1,423
Prepaid Expenses & Other Receivables	$1,367	$1,515	$1,579
Total Current Assets	**$27,006**	**$25,784**	**$22,247**
Total Property, Plant & Equipment	$16,438	$15,948	$14,645
Less Accumulated Depreciation	$9,304	$8,937	$8,055
Property, Plant & Equipment, Net	$7,134	$7,010	$6,590
Other Assets			
Net Intangible Assets	$11,556	$11,834	$11,022
Goodwill	$9,701	$9,491	$8,991
Deferred Taxes on Income	$2,462	$1,476	$1,527
Other	$1,979	$1,405	$1,952
Total Assets	**$59,838**	**$57,000**	**$52,329**
LIABILITIES AND SHAREHOLDER EQUITY			
Current Liabilities			
Loans & Notes Payable	$3,141	$1,582	$1,914
Accounts Payable	$2,991	$3,318	$2,471

(*Continued*)

Table C.5:   (*Continued*)

	2015	2014	2013
Accrued Liabilities	$2,427	$2,849	$3,031
Accrued Rebates, Returns & Promotions	$2,440	$1,743	$1,305
Accrued Compensation & Employee-Related Obligations	$1,110	$1,196	$1,102
Accrued Taxes on Income	$336	$217	$304
Total Current Liabilities	**$12,445**	**$10,905**	**$10,126**
Long-Term Debt	$5,767	$6,574	$5,256
Deferred Taxes on Income	$1,149	$1,371	$1,573
Employee-Related Obligations	$3,971	$4,335	$3,070
Other Liabilities	$4,593	$3,493	$3,098
Total Liabilities	**$27,926**	**$26,677**	**$23,123**
Shareholders' Equity			
Common Stock	$1,399	$1,356	$1,231
Employee Benefit Plans	−$2,376	−$2,746	−$1,187
Gains on Financial Transactions	−$3,528	−$1,915	$59
Accumulated Other Comprehensive Income	−$5,905	−$4,661	−$1,128
Retained Earnings	$46,592	$42,274	$35,295
Total Shareholders' Equity	**$31,913**	**$30,322**	**$29,206**

Note: All figures are in millions of dollars.

acquisition through existing capital. Cash flow needed to be examined very carefully (see Table C.6). At this point in time, the financial markets were not looking favorably at BPC's capital structure and Clayton knew that he needed at least $2 billion to fund the immunotherapy transaction. If he was unable to fund the new acquisition, the Board's targets for earnings and free cash flow would not be met, and that would surely cost him his job.

While he had every intention to honor the pledge he made on behalf of his firm, Clayton's options going forward were rather few. If Garcia and

Table C.6:   BPC Financials: Cash Flow Statement

	2015	2014	2013
Net Earnings	**$6,911**	**$7,096**	**$5,455**
Depreciation & Amortization of Property & Intangibles	$1,680	$1,693	$1,619
Stock-based Compensation	$392	$344	$287
Venezuela Adjustments	$55	$38	$43
Asset Write-downs & Impairments	$280	$178	$291
Net Loss (Gain) on Sale of Assets/Businesses	−$1,159	−$1,036	−$45
Net Loss (Gain) on Equity Investment Transactions	—	—	−$164
Deferred Tax Provision	−$121	$192	−$239
Accounts Receivable Allowances	$8	−$12	−$52
Accounts Receivable	−$194	−$107	−$249
Inventories	−$201	−$487	−$245
Accounts Payable & Accrued Liabilities	−$1	$415	$718
Other Current & Non-current Assets	$29	$192	−$668
Other Current & Non-current Liabilities	$968	−$476	$118
Net Cash Flows from Operating Activities	**$8,647**	**$8,030**	**$6,868**
Additions to Property, Plant & Equipment	−$1,553	−$1,615	−$1,418
Proceeds from the Disposal of Assets/Businesses, Net	$1,554	$2,013	$181
Acquisitions, Net of Cash Acquired	−$428	−$926	−$329
Purchases of Investments	−$18,312	−$15,177	−$7,463
Sales of Investments	$15,317	$10,485	$7,122
Other Investing Activities (Primarily Intangibles)	−$46	−$130	−$105
Net Cash Flows from Investing Activities	**−$3,469**	**−$5,349**	**−$2,013**
Dividends to Shareholders	−$3,666	−$3,377	−$2,874
Repurchase of Common Stock	−$2,373	−$3,097	−$1,395
Proceeds from Short-Term Debt	$1,084	$810	$556
Retirement of Short-Term Debt	−$468	−$551	−$551
Proceeds from Long-Term Debt	$34	$912	$1,423
Retirement of Long-Term Debt	−$30	−$802	−$628

(*Continued*)

Table C.6: *(Continued)*

	2015	2014	2013
Proceeds from the Exercise of Stock Options/ Excess Tax Benefits	$581	$775	$1,045
Other Financing Activities	−$26	—	$22
Net Cash Flows from Financing Activities	**−$4,865**	**−$5,330**	**−$2,402**
Effect of Exchange Rate Changes on Cash & Cash Equivalents	−$668	−$135	−$80
Increase in Cash & Cash Equivalents	−$355	−$2,784	$2,373
Cash & Cash Equivalents, Beginning of Year	**$6,514**	**$9,097**	**$5,881**
Cash & Cash Equivalents, End of year	**$6,159**	**$6,313**	**$8,253**
Cash Paid during the Year for Interest	$277	$262	$235
Cash Paid During the Year for Interest, Net of Amount Capitalized	$231	$212	$194
Cash Paid during the Year for Income Taxes	$1,285	$1,537	$1,244

Note: All figures are in millions of dollars.

Moore were not able to forge a satisfactory solution, which was adopted by the suppliers, Clayton might have to consider doing a "180" on his pledge. Clayton was fully aware that there was also considerable risk to that option, as it could set off a public relations nightmare. If he ignored the pledge he signed, local politicians and the public would be outraged, and the crisis over his lack of integrity might cost him the last bit of trust he had with the Board of Directors, and ultimately his job. At this point, all he could do was hope that his leadership team might find a way.

Index